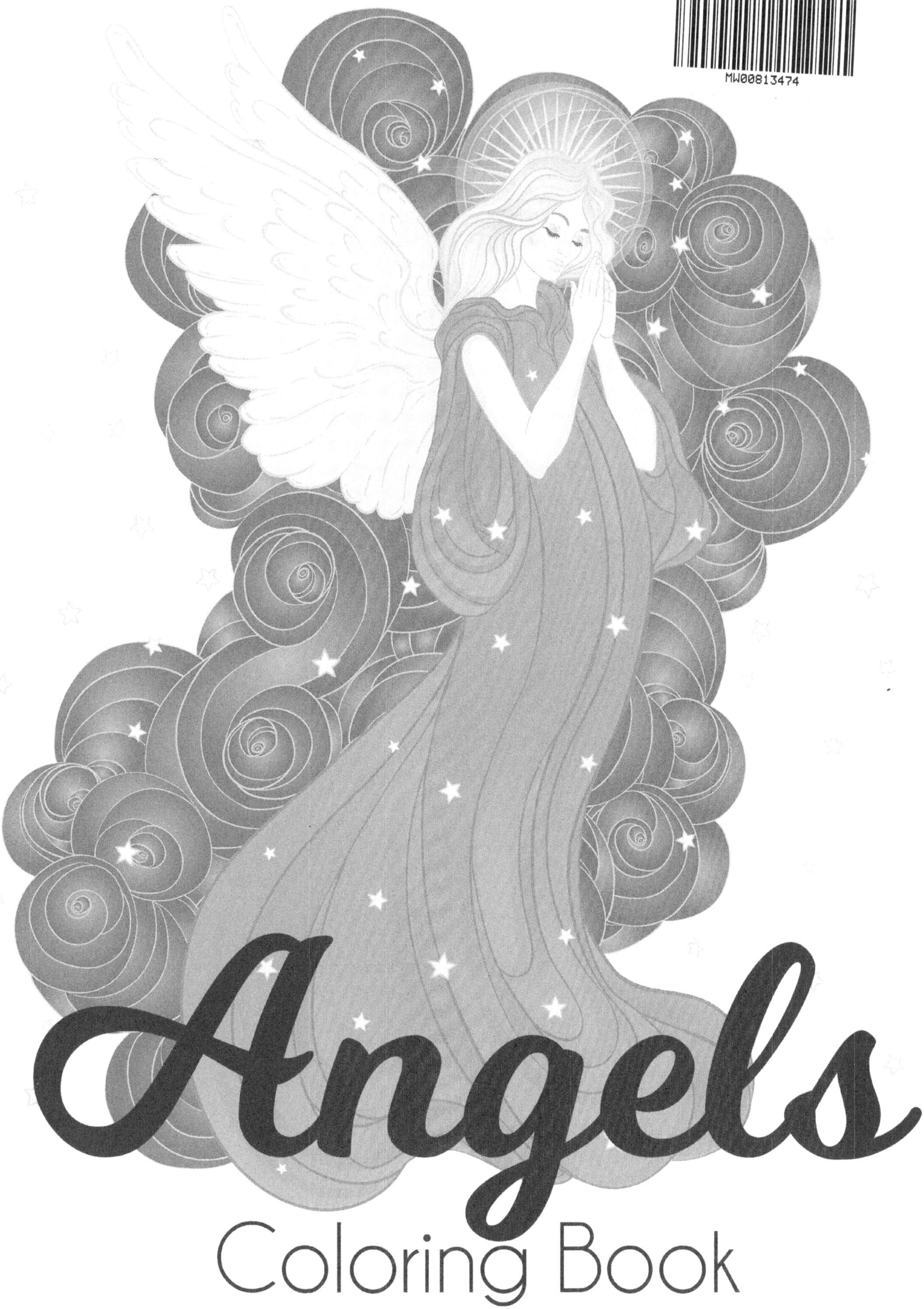

Angels

Coloring Book

Preview of Coloring Pages

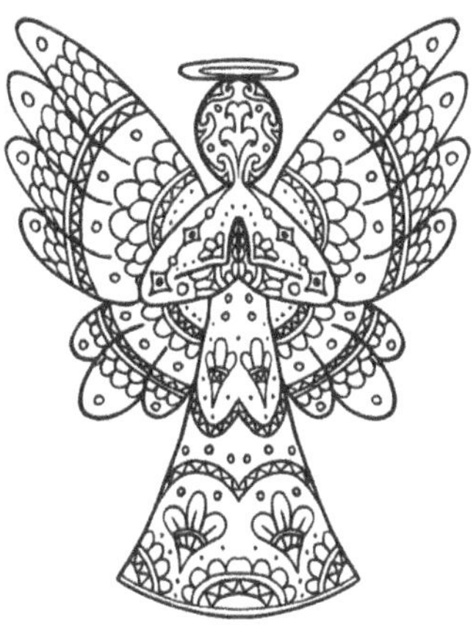
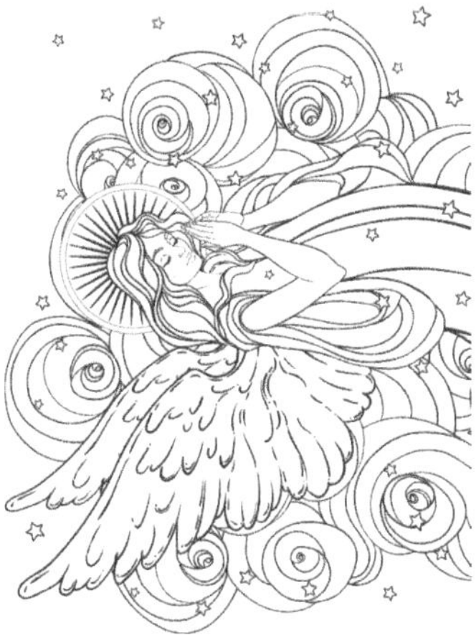
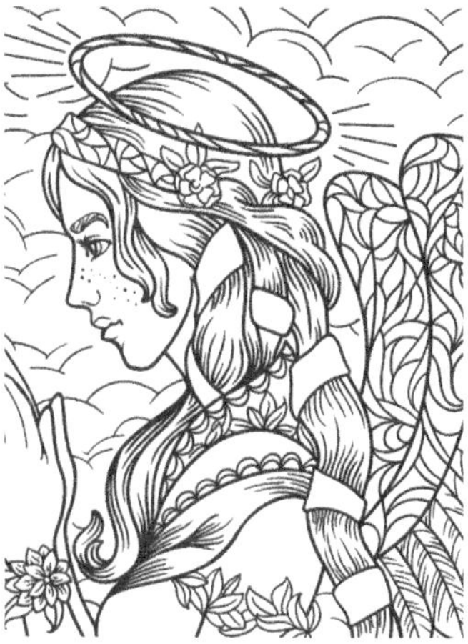
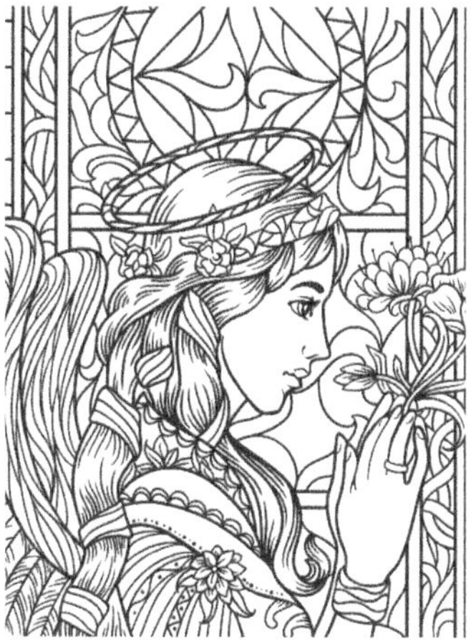
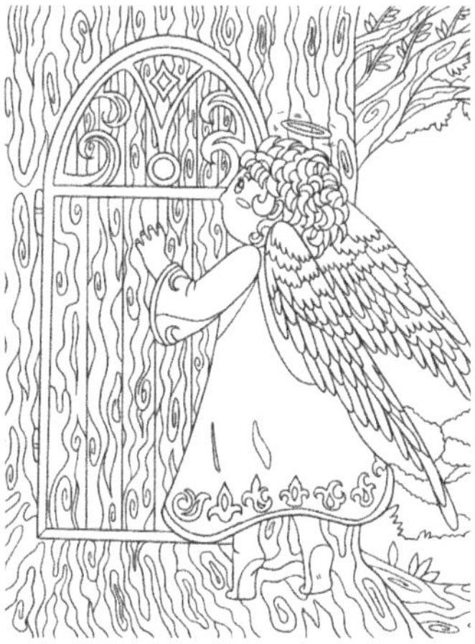
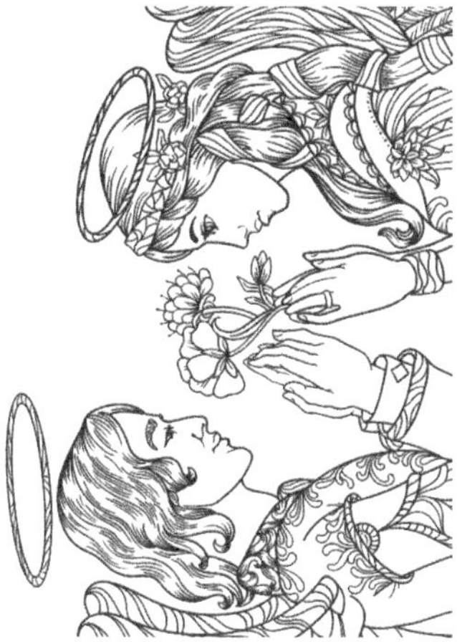
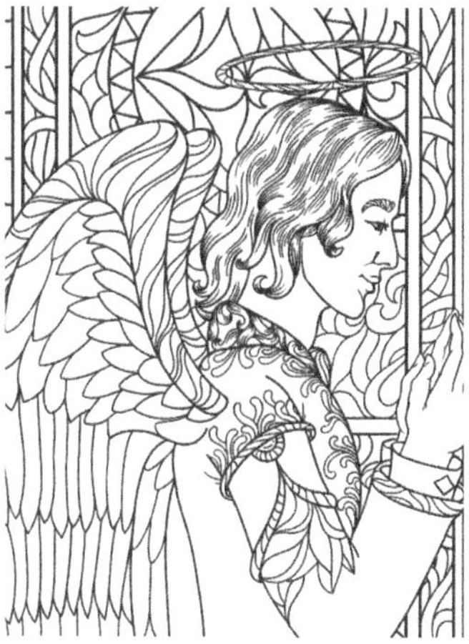
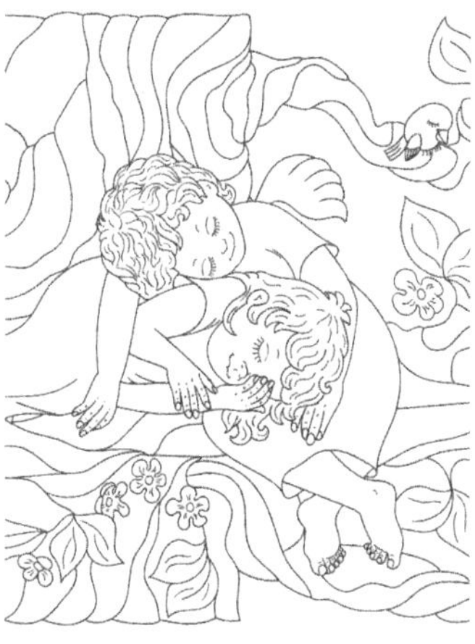
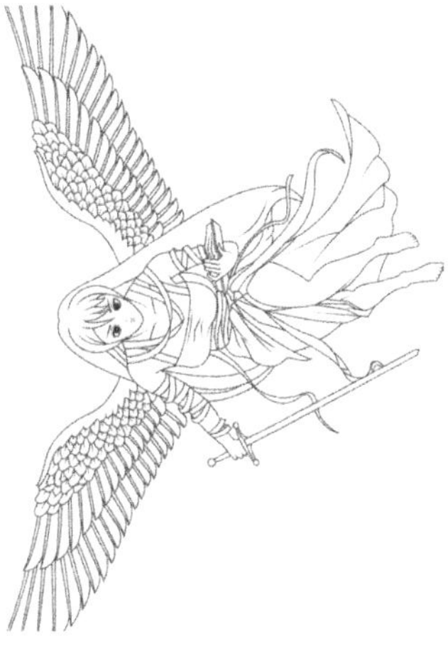
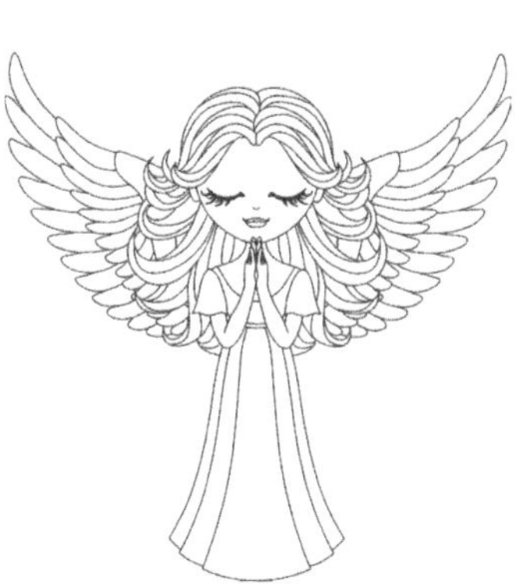
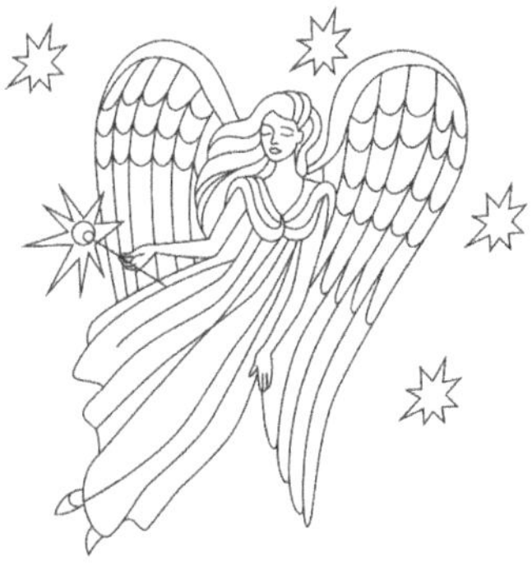
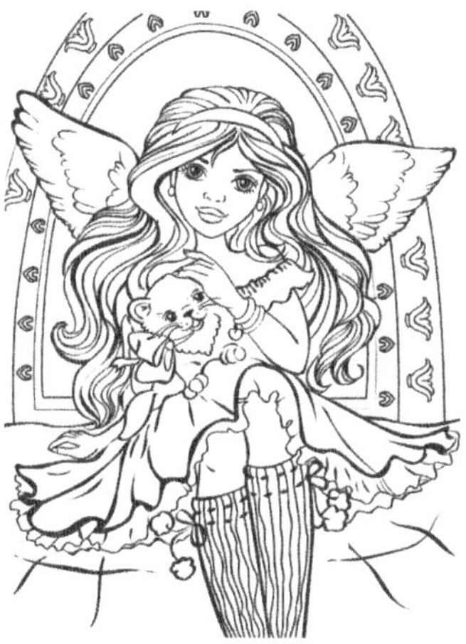
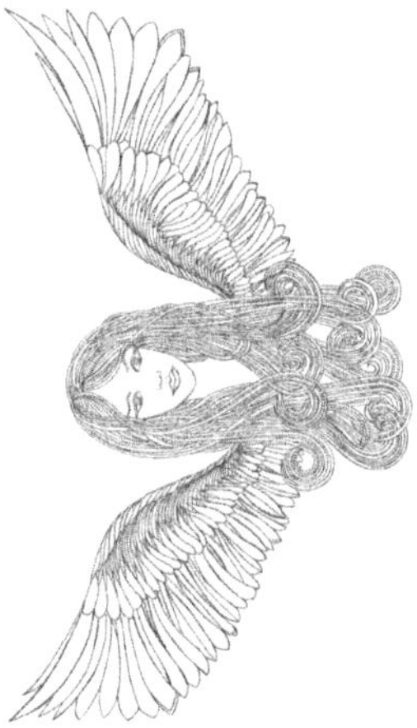
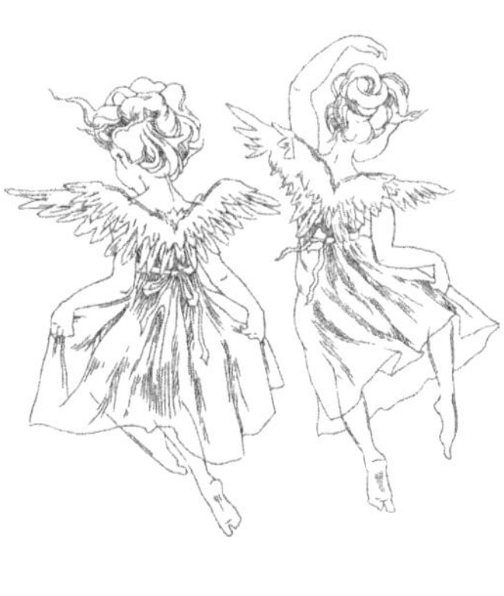
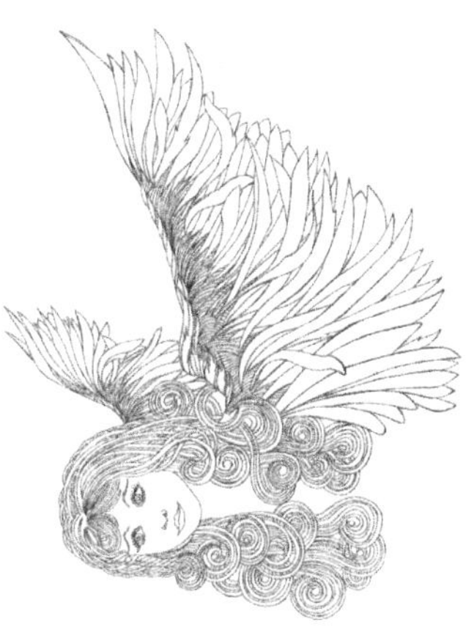
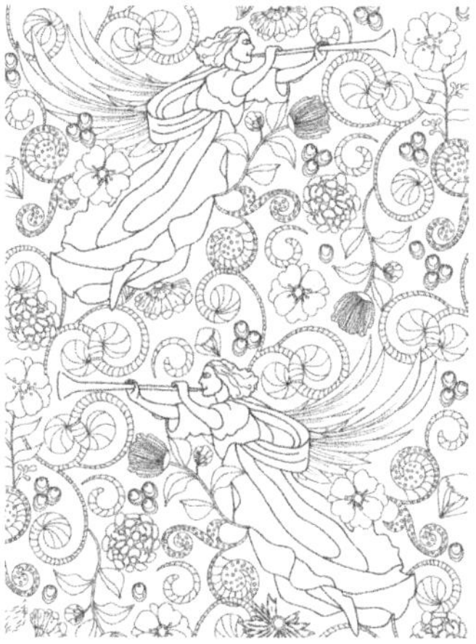

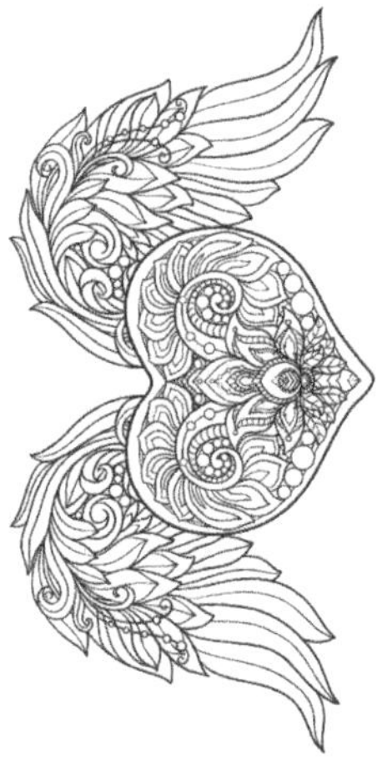
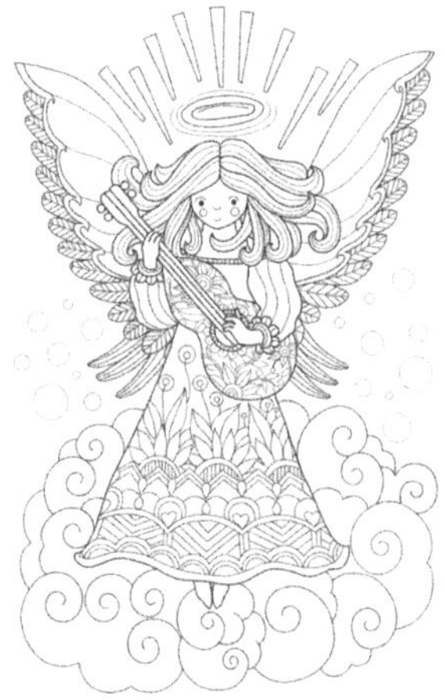
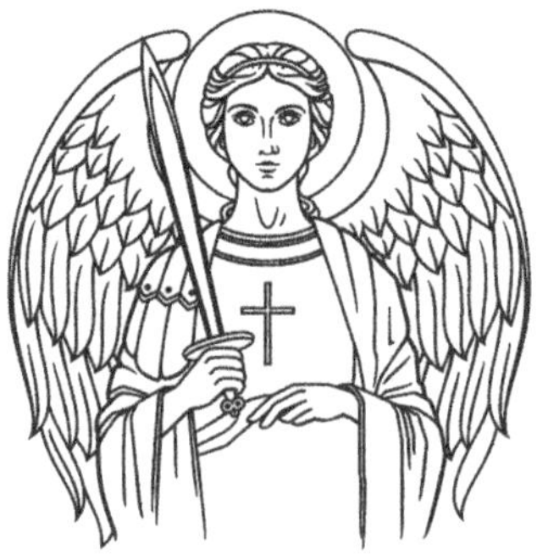
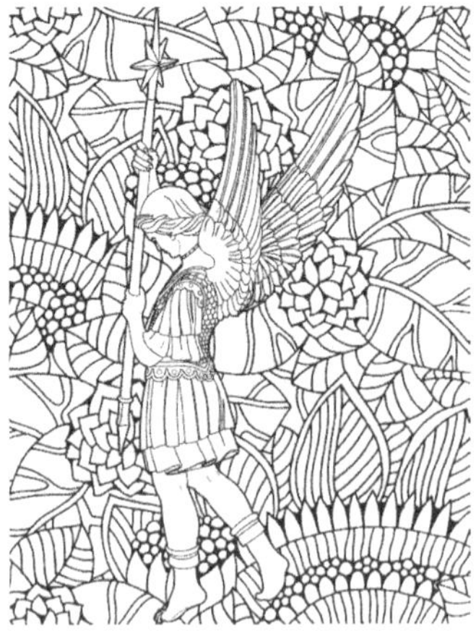
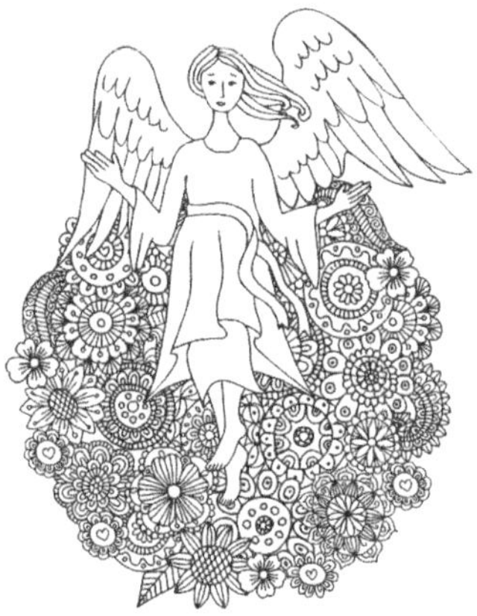
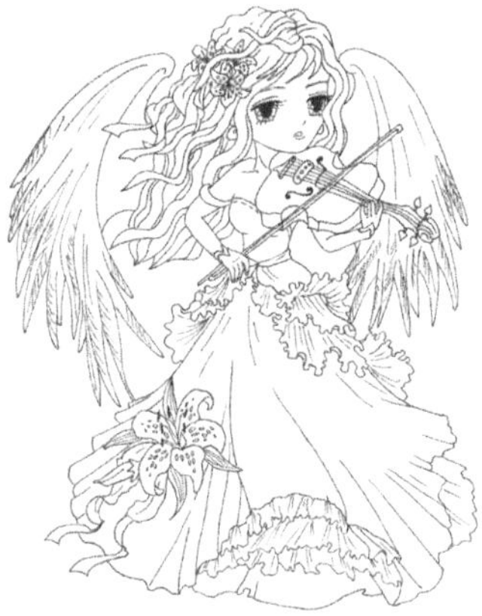
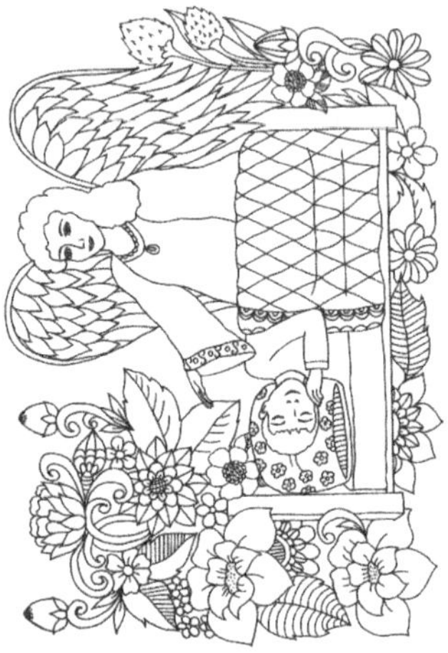
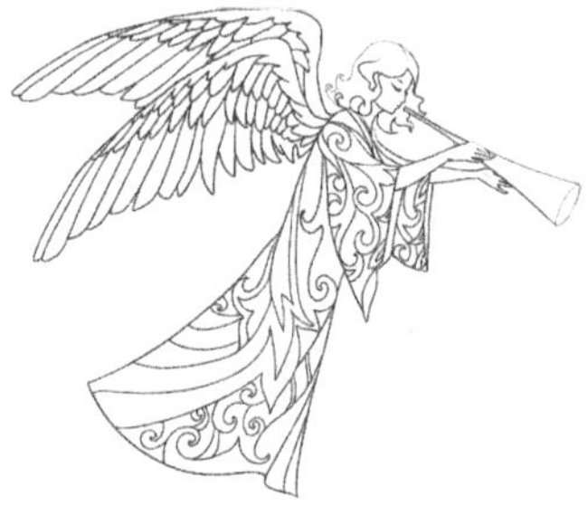
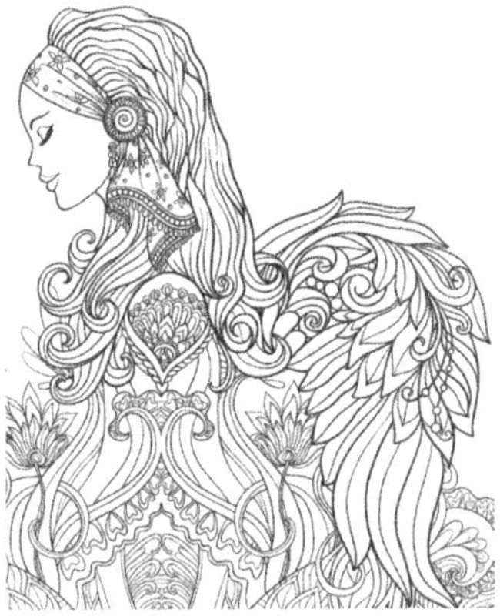
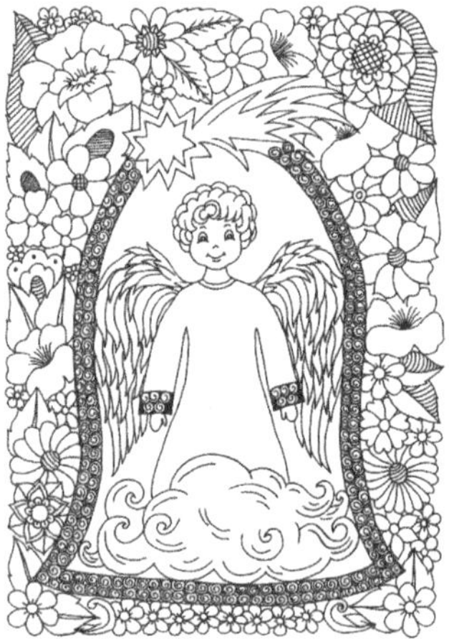
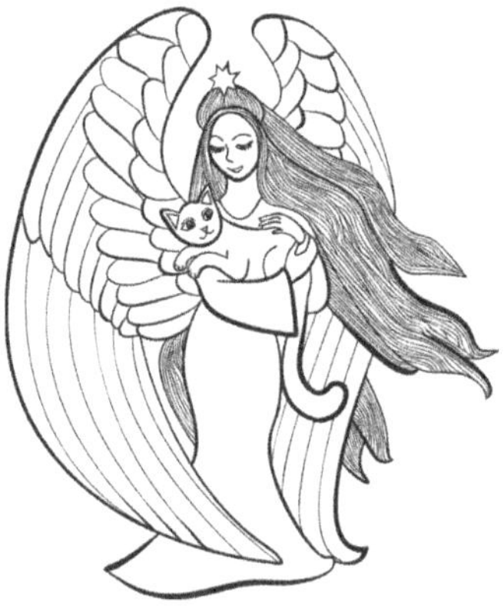
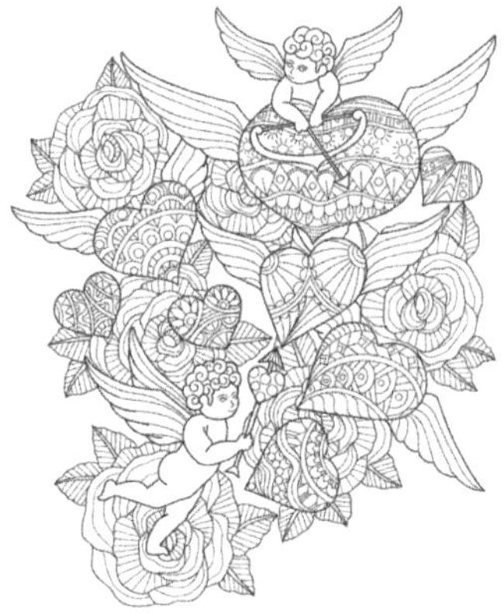
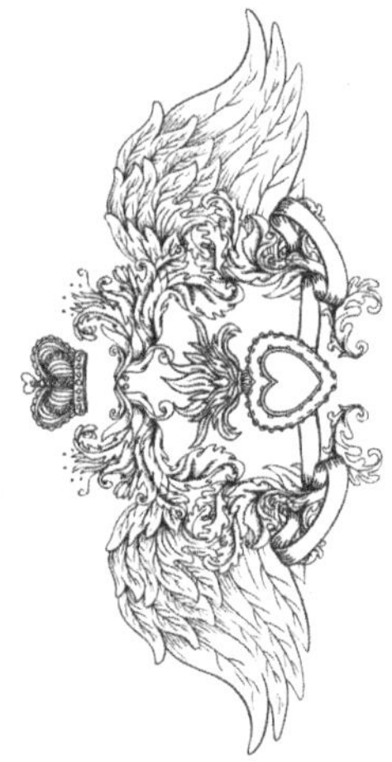
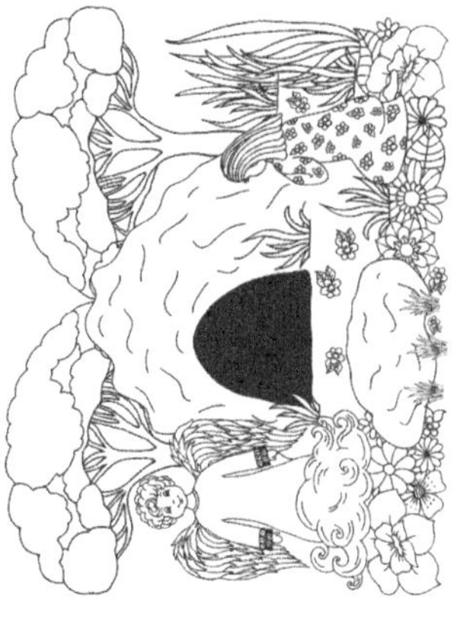
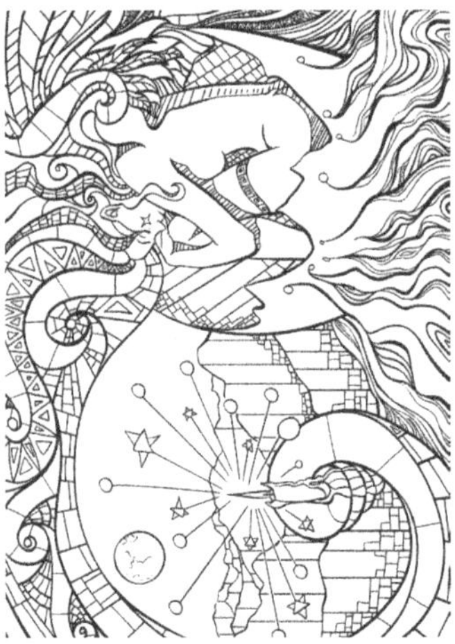
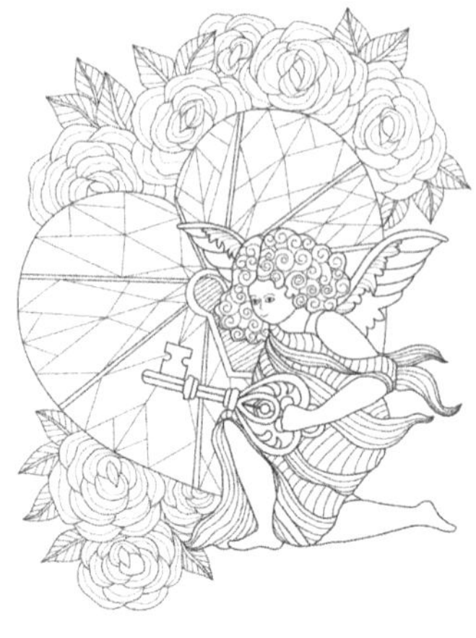

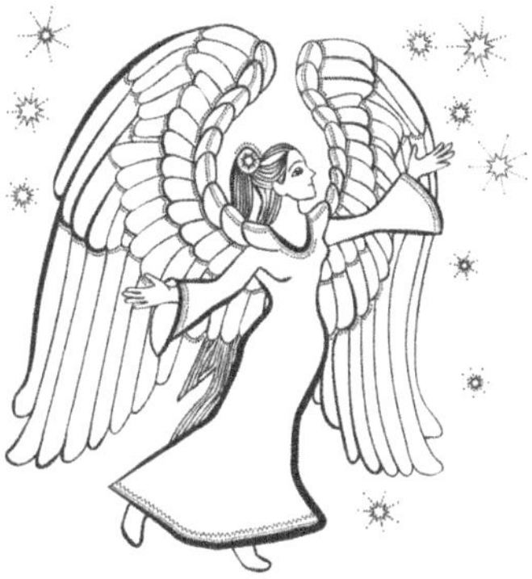
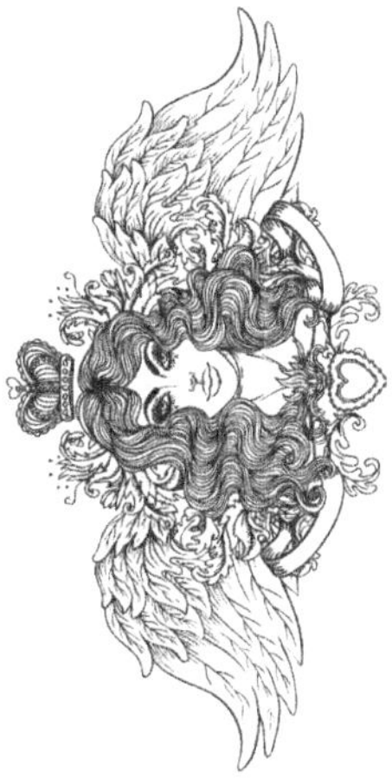
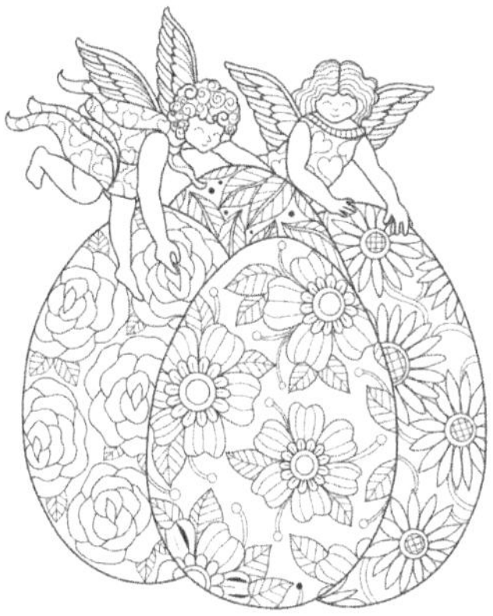
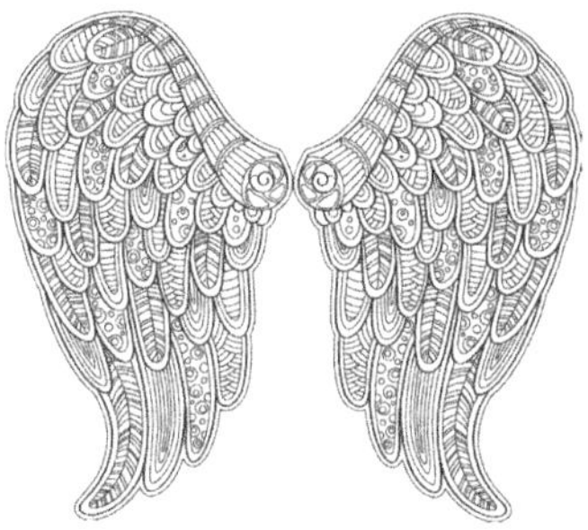
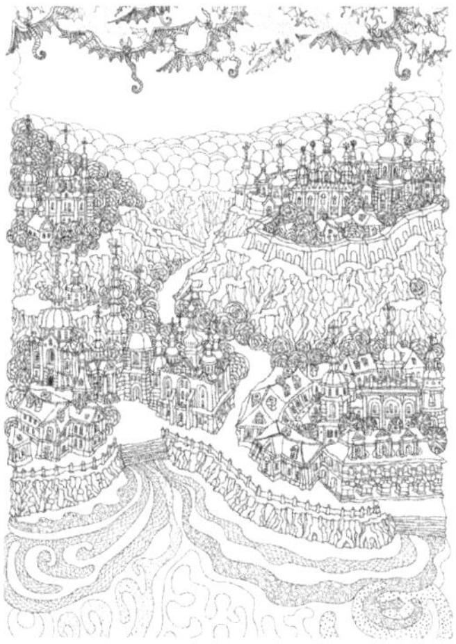
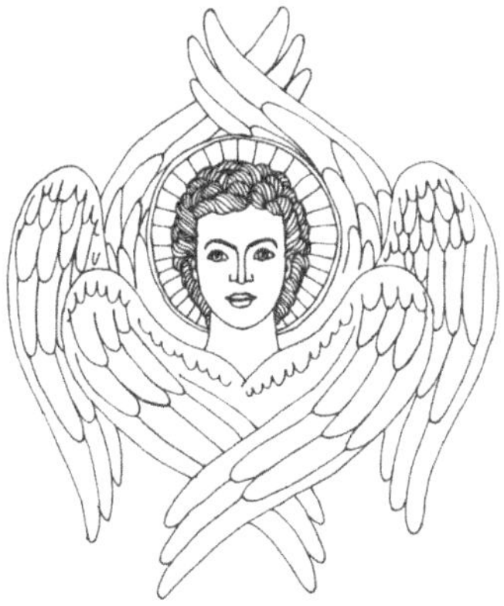
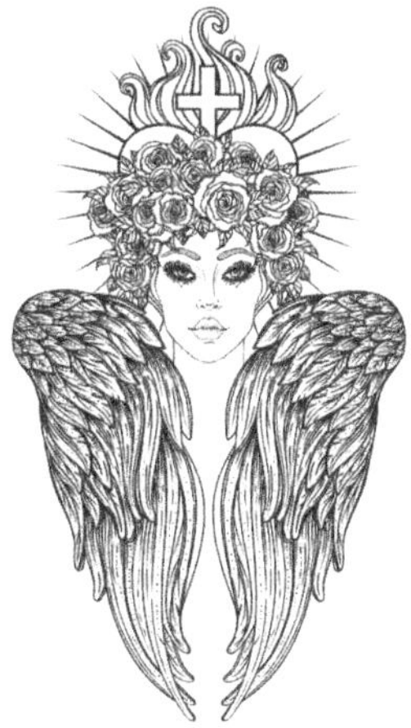
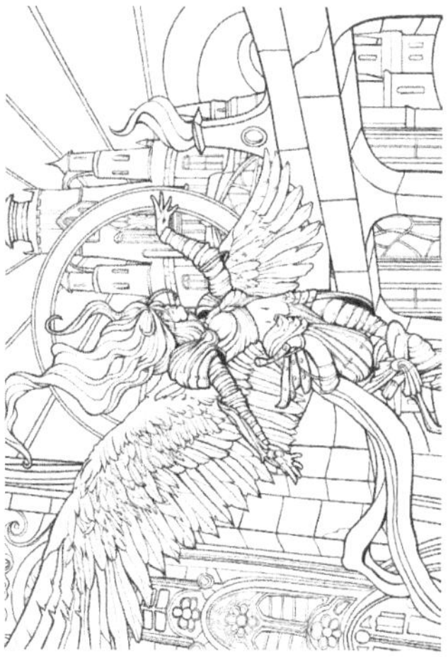
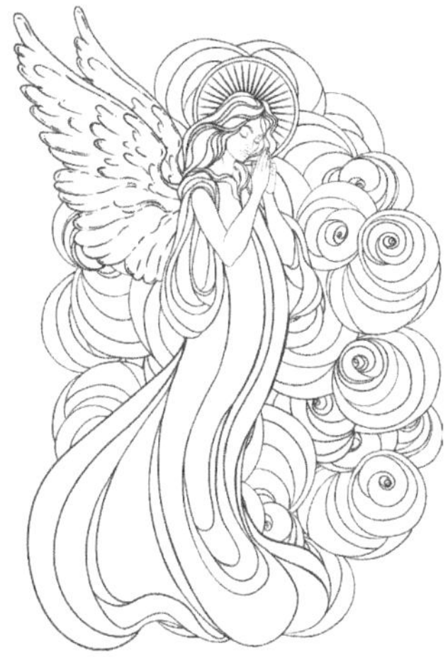
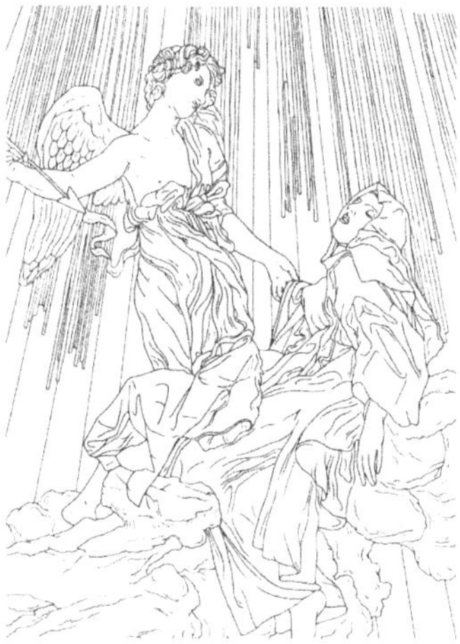
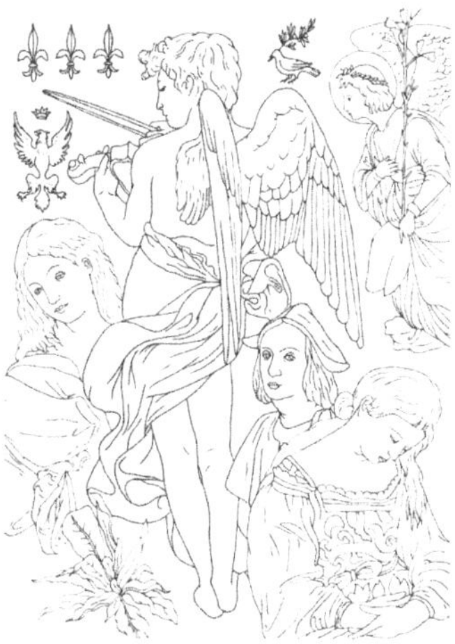
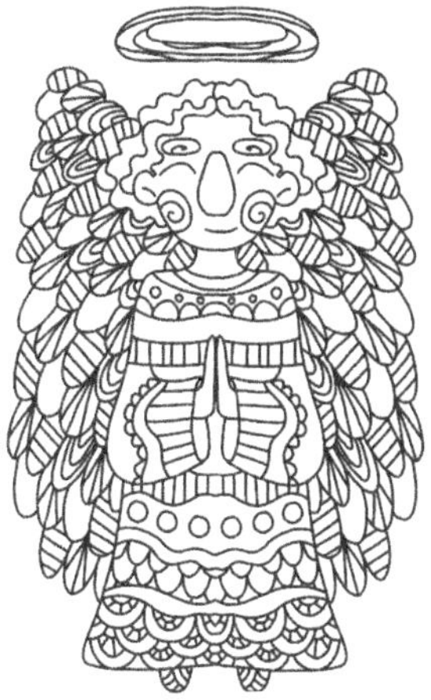

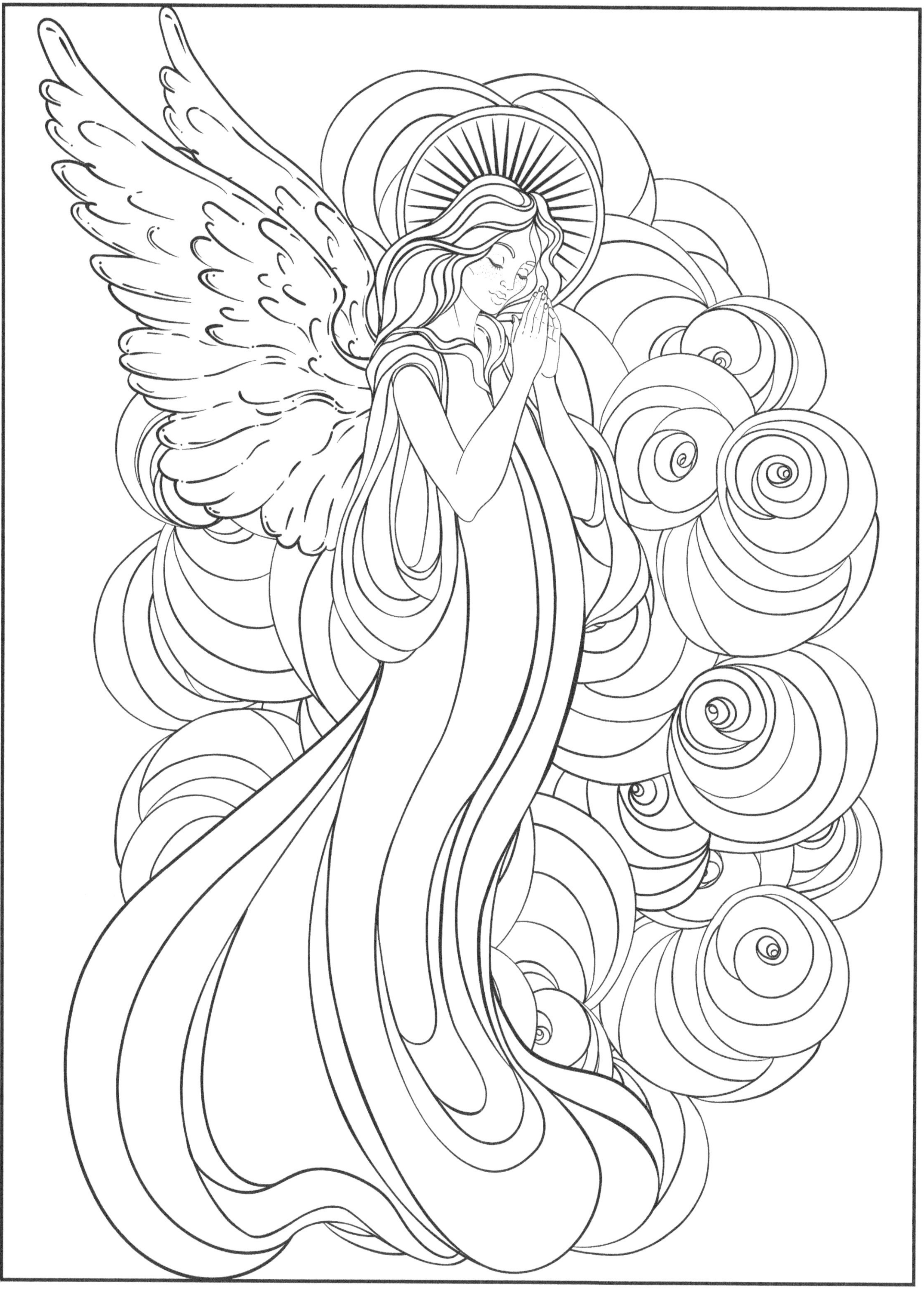

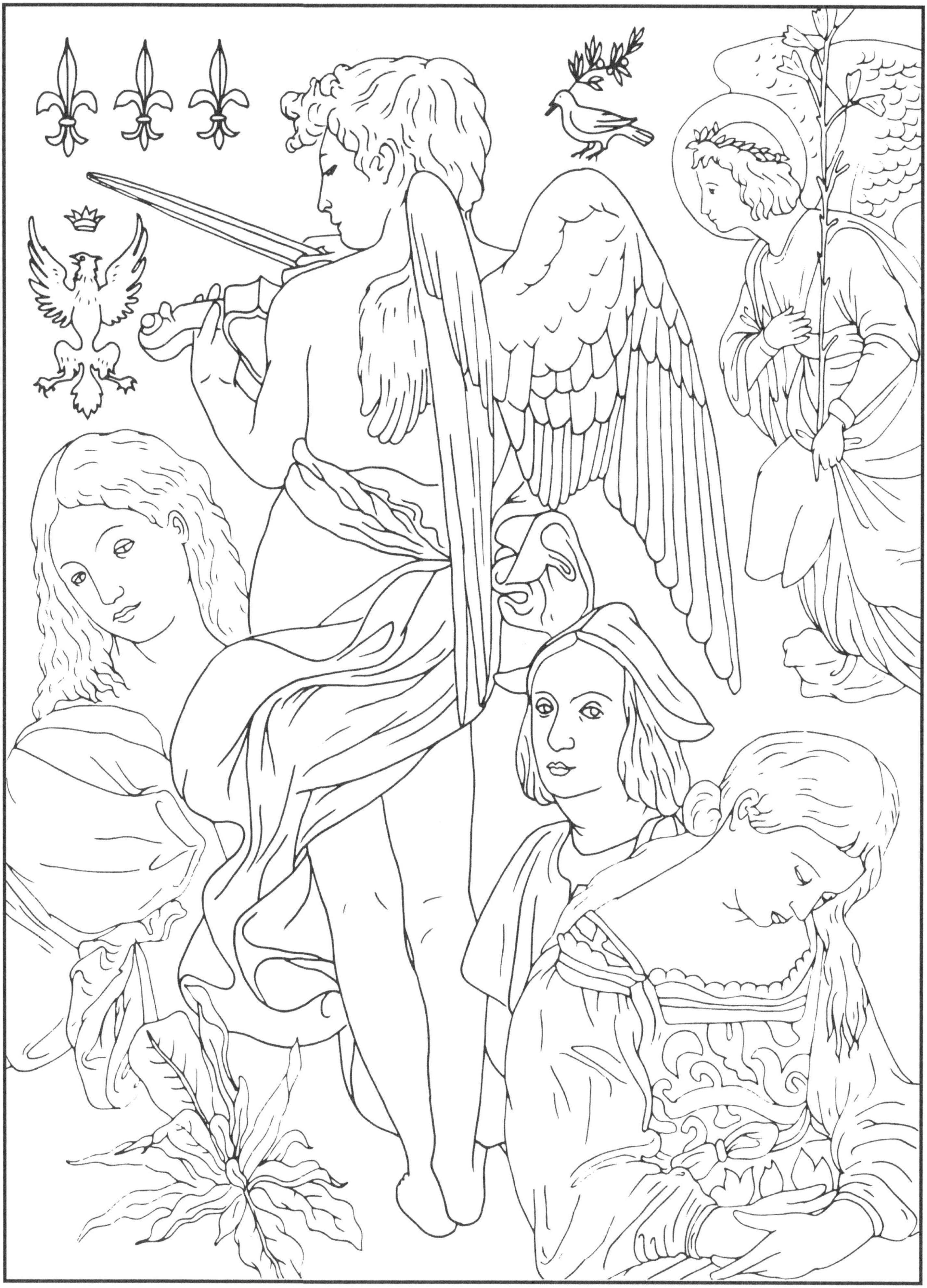

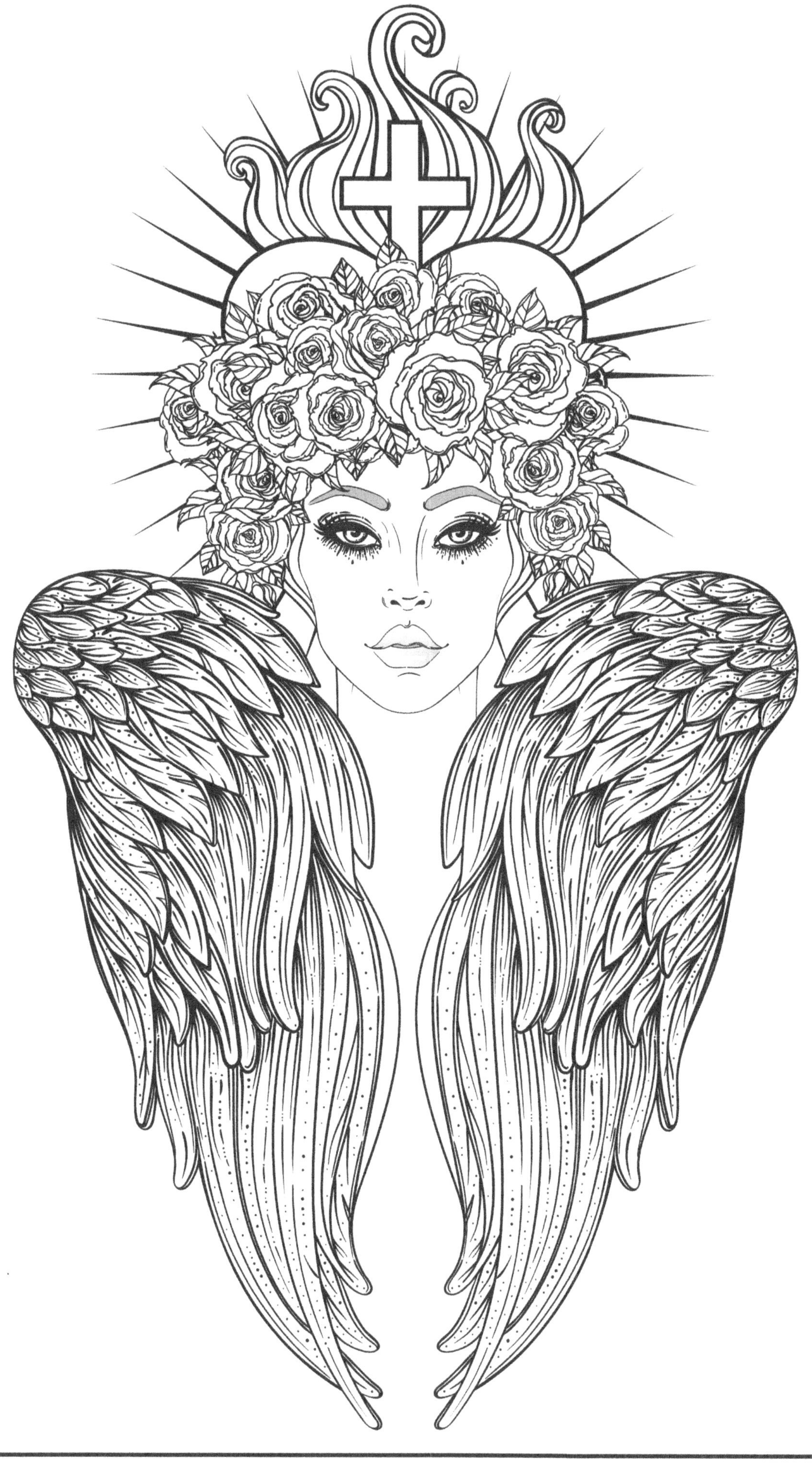

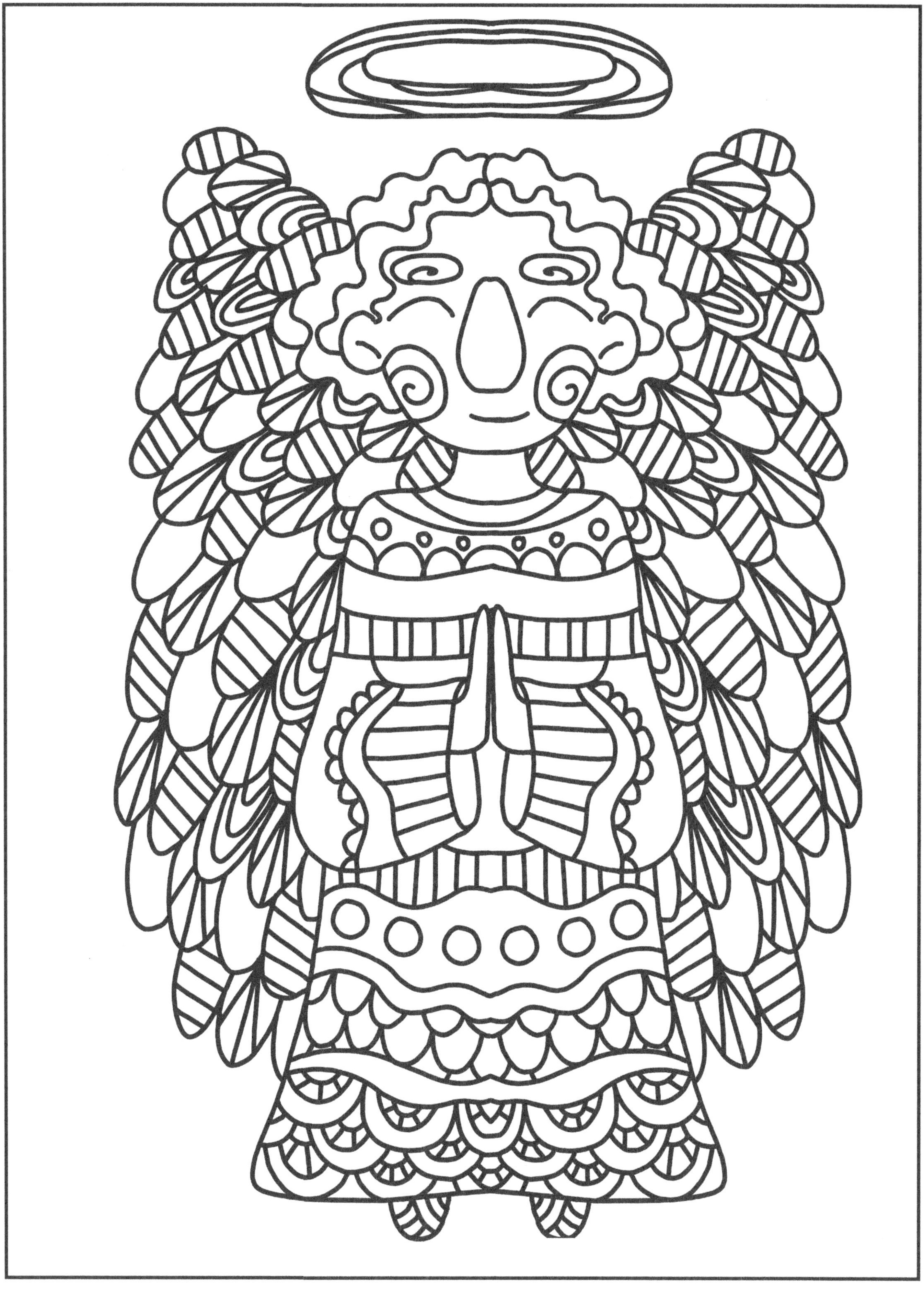

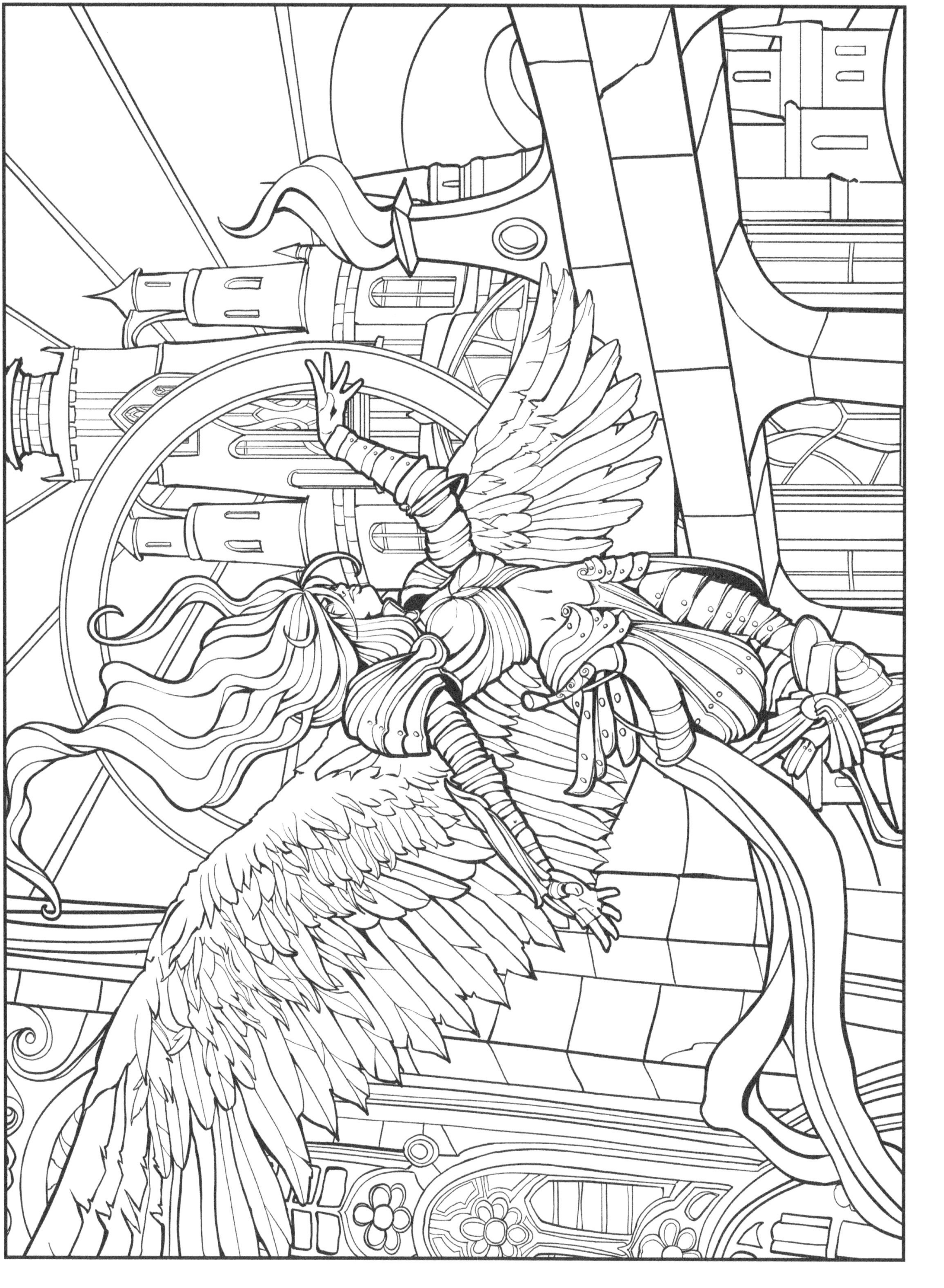

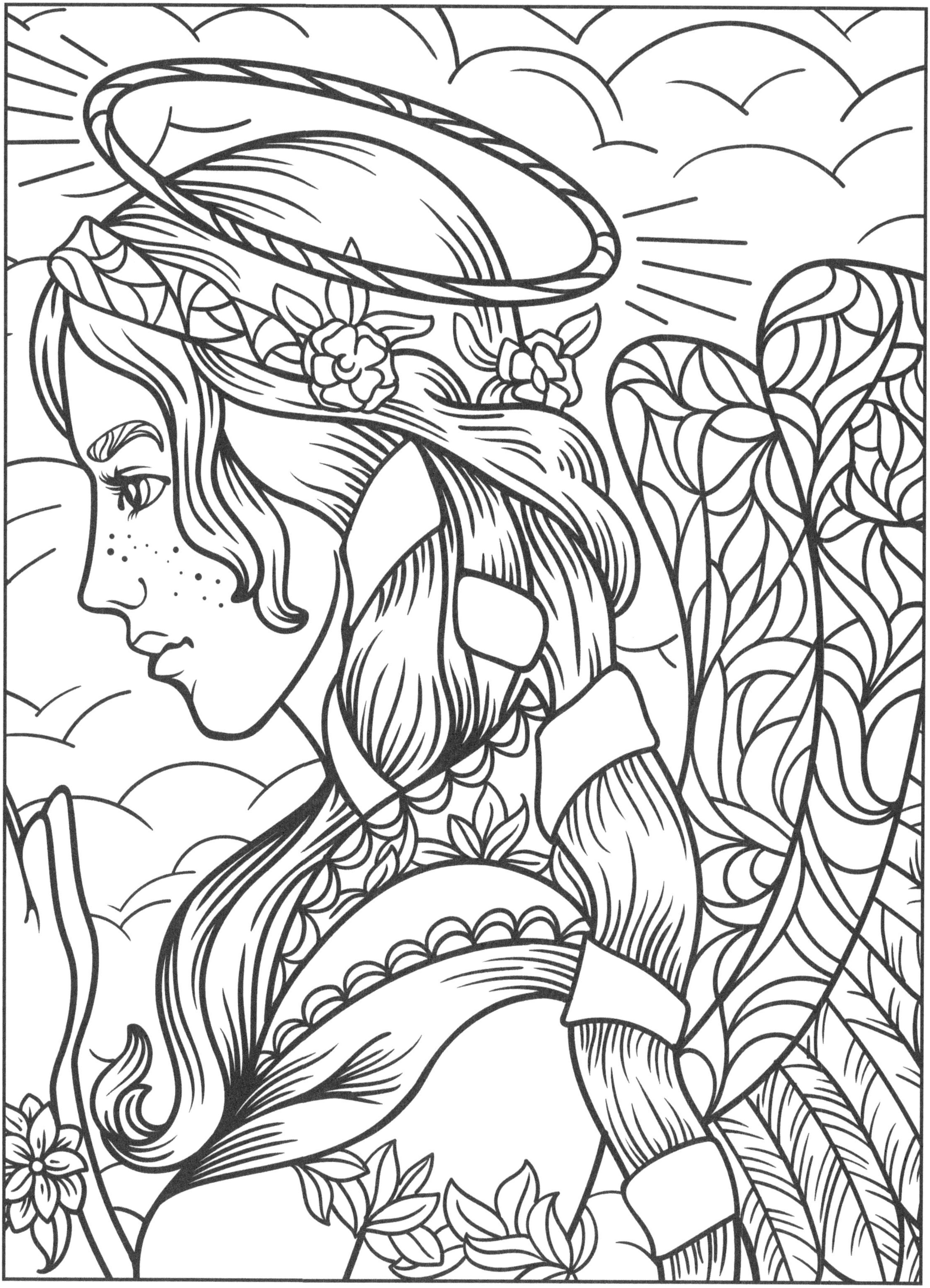

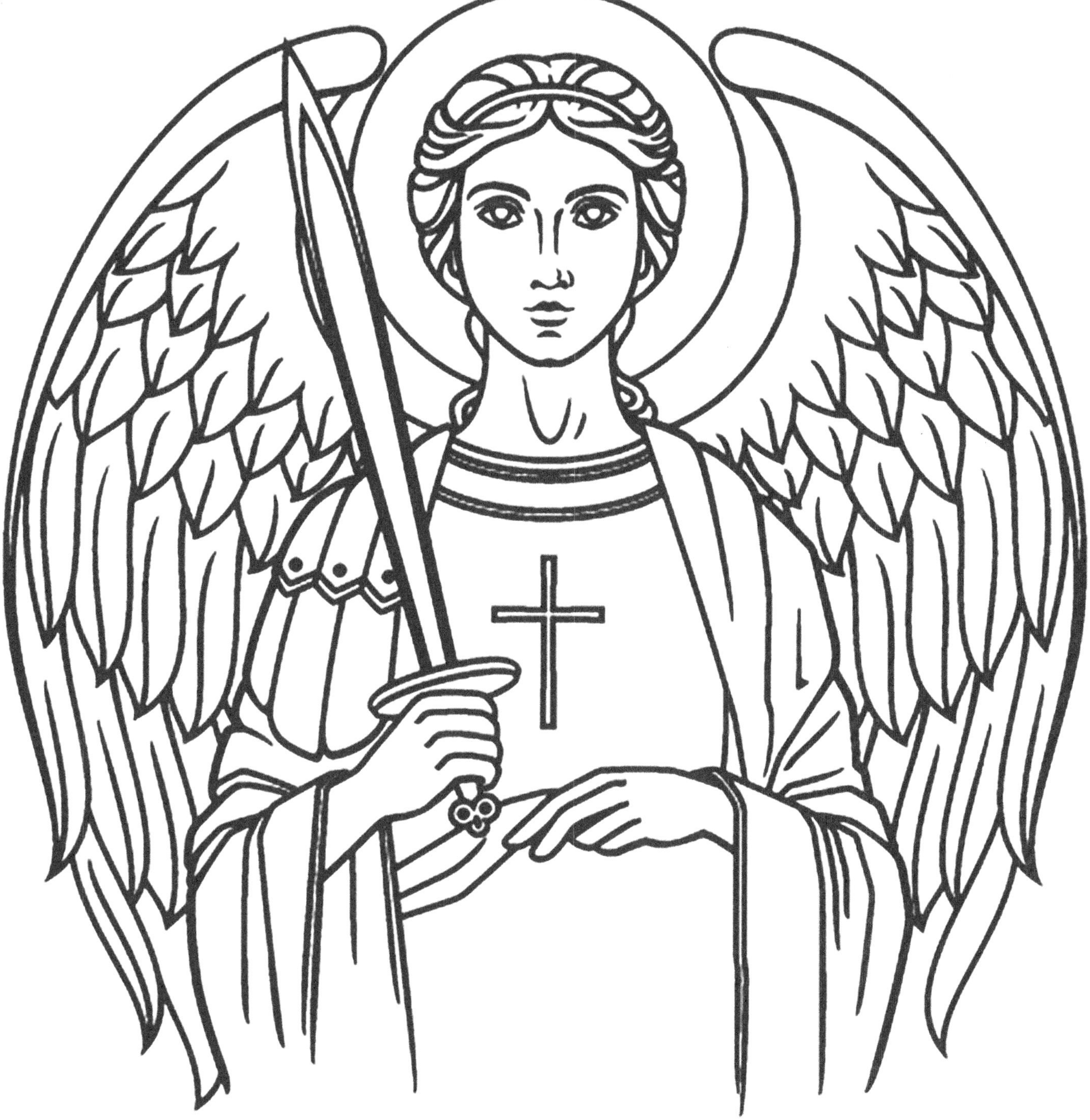

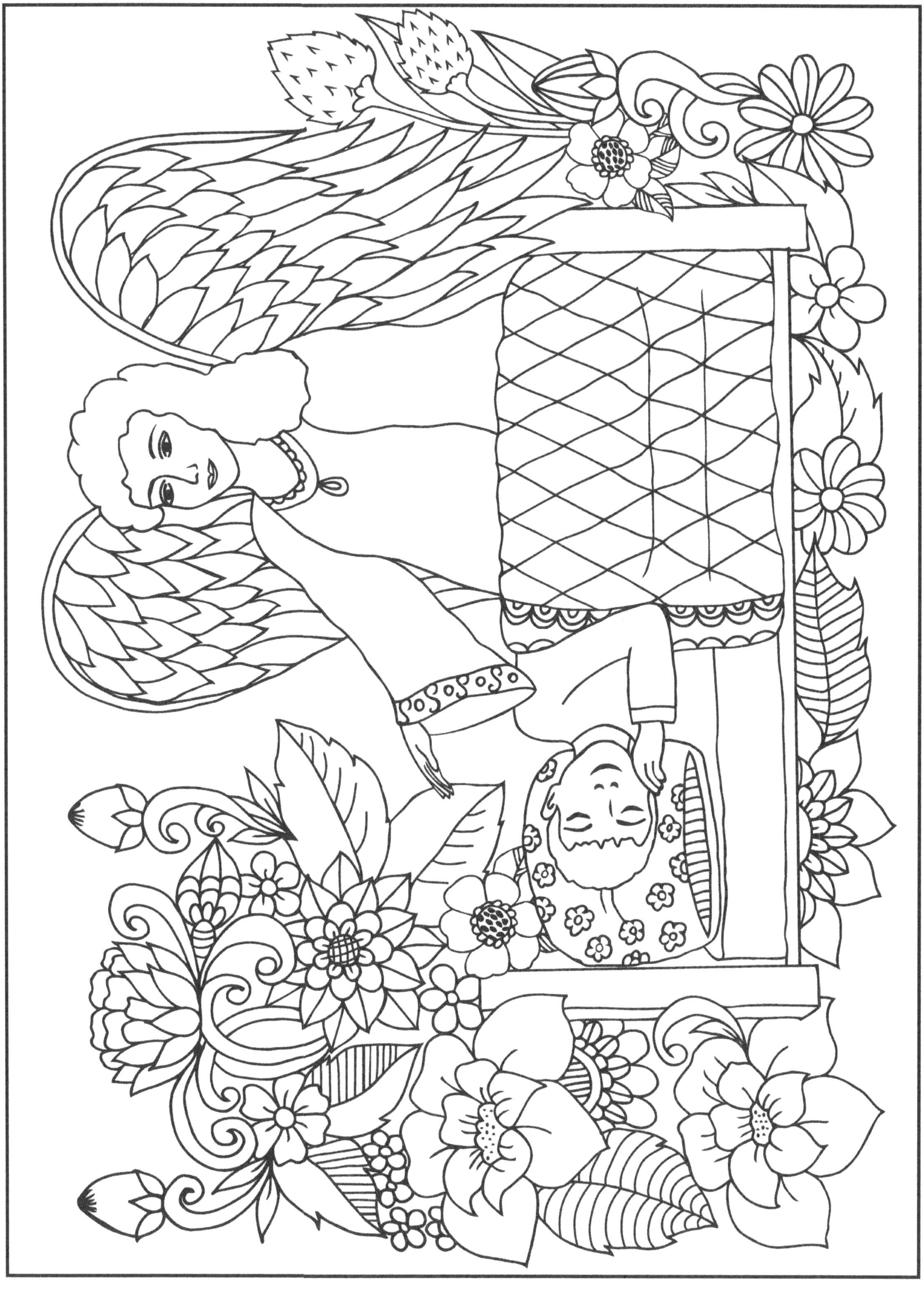

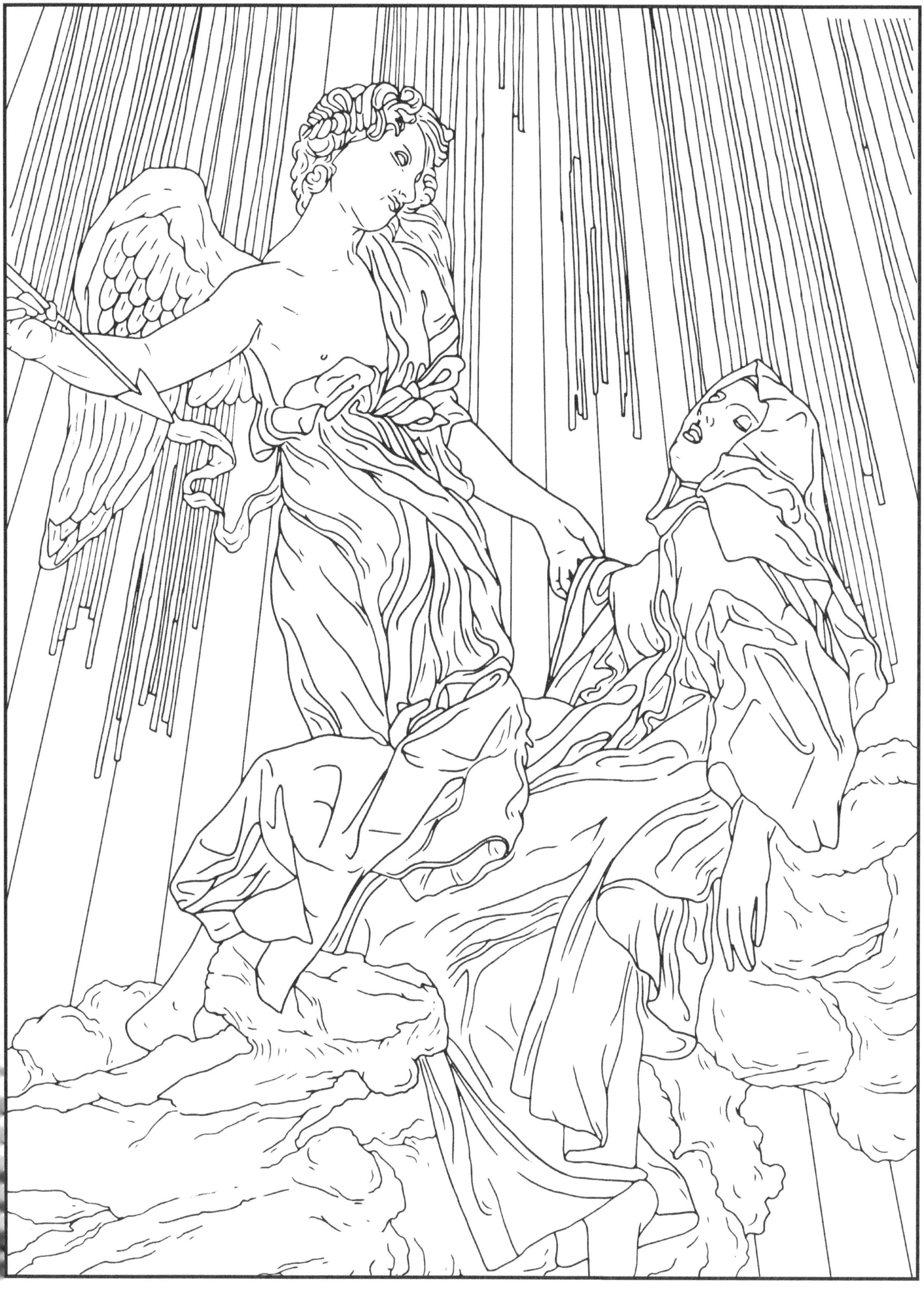

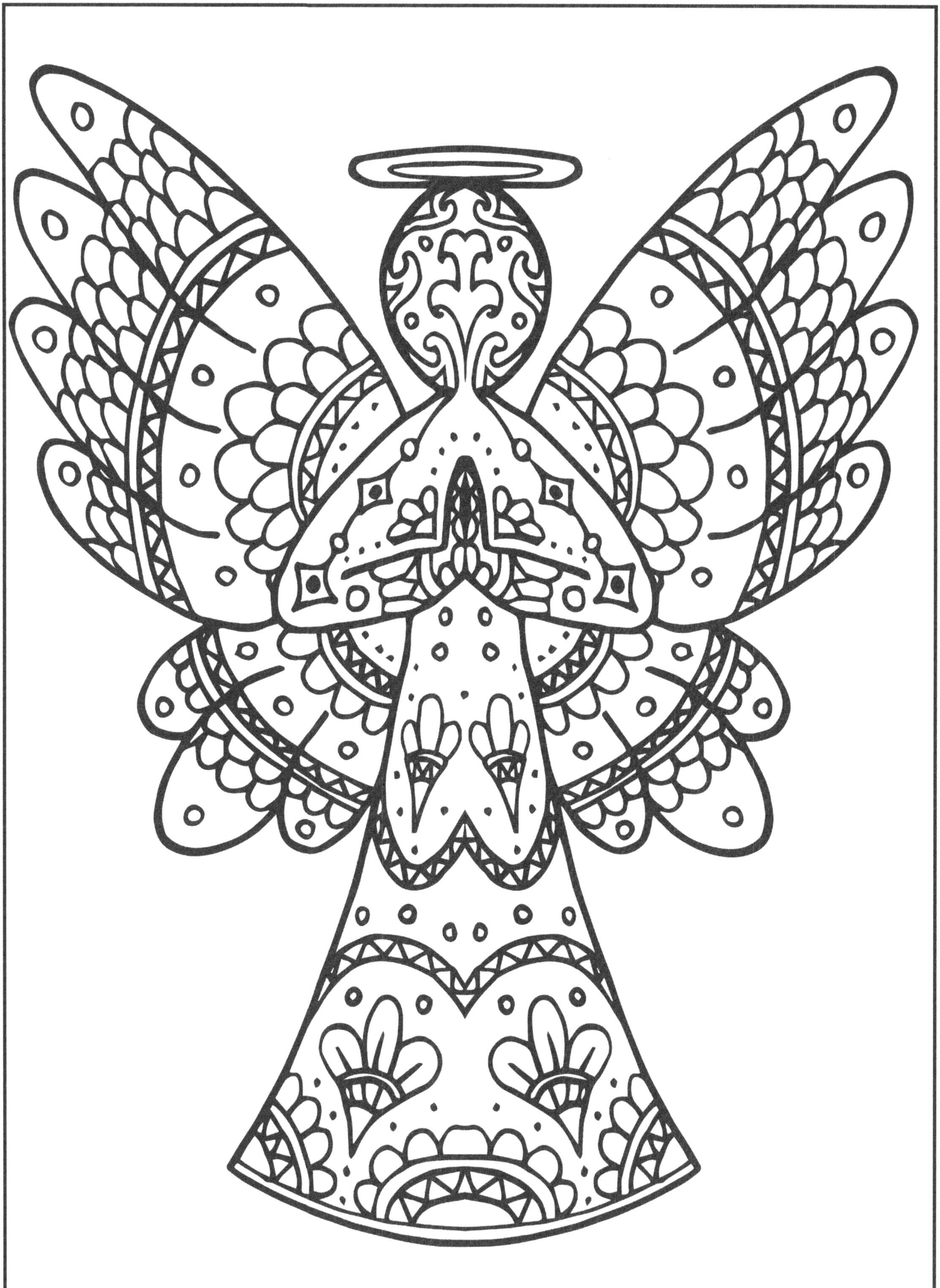

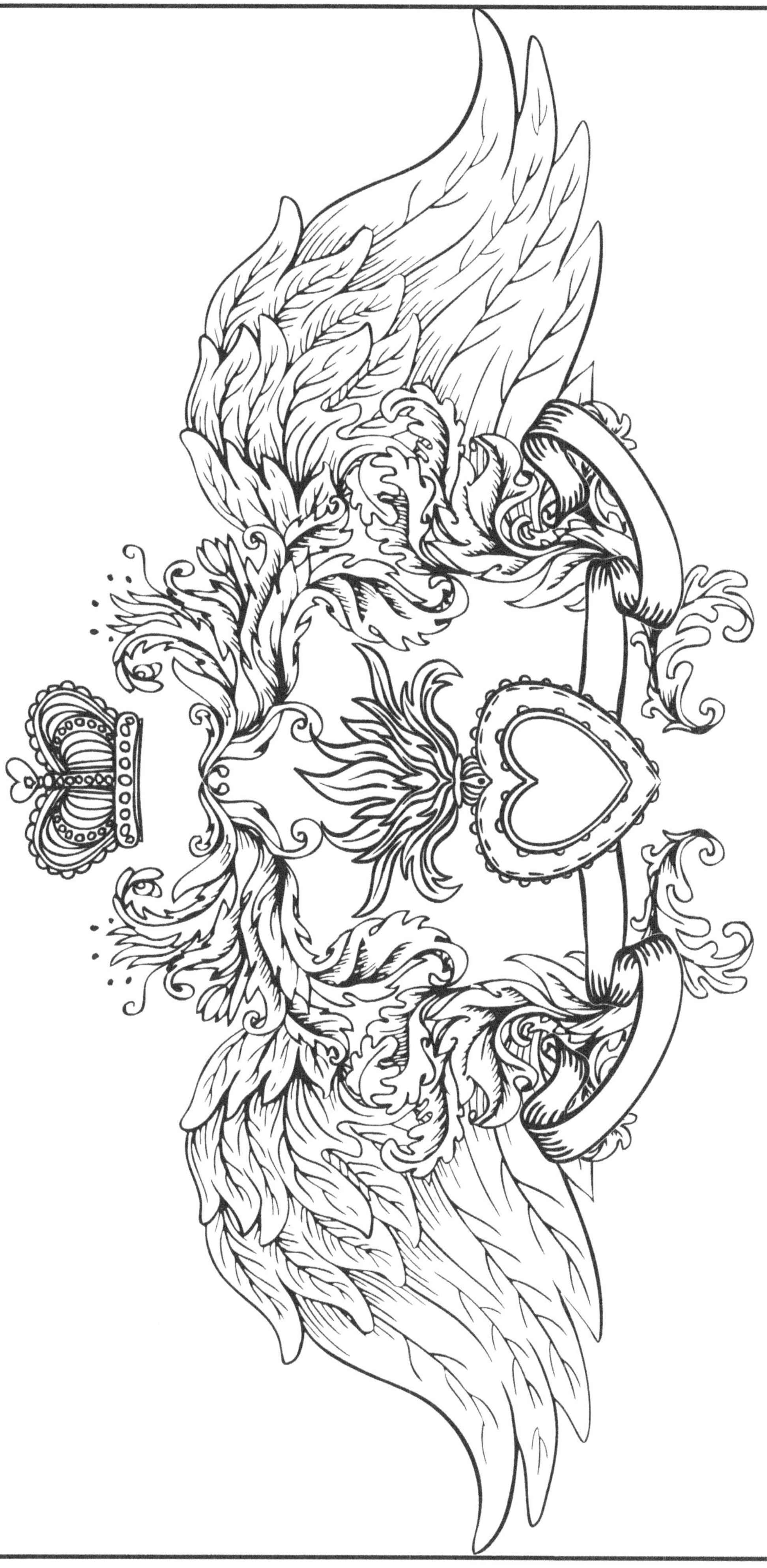

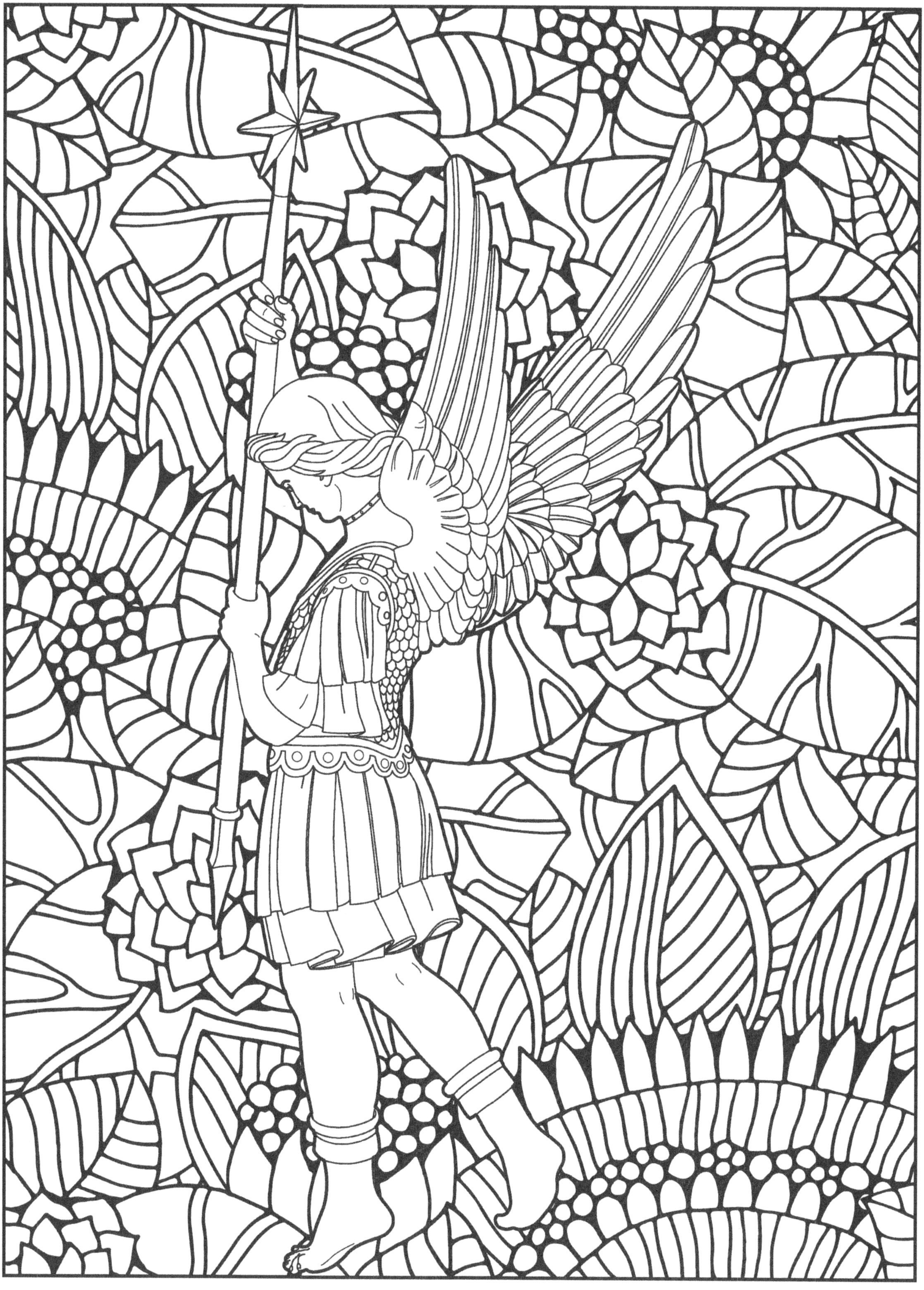

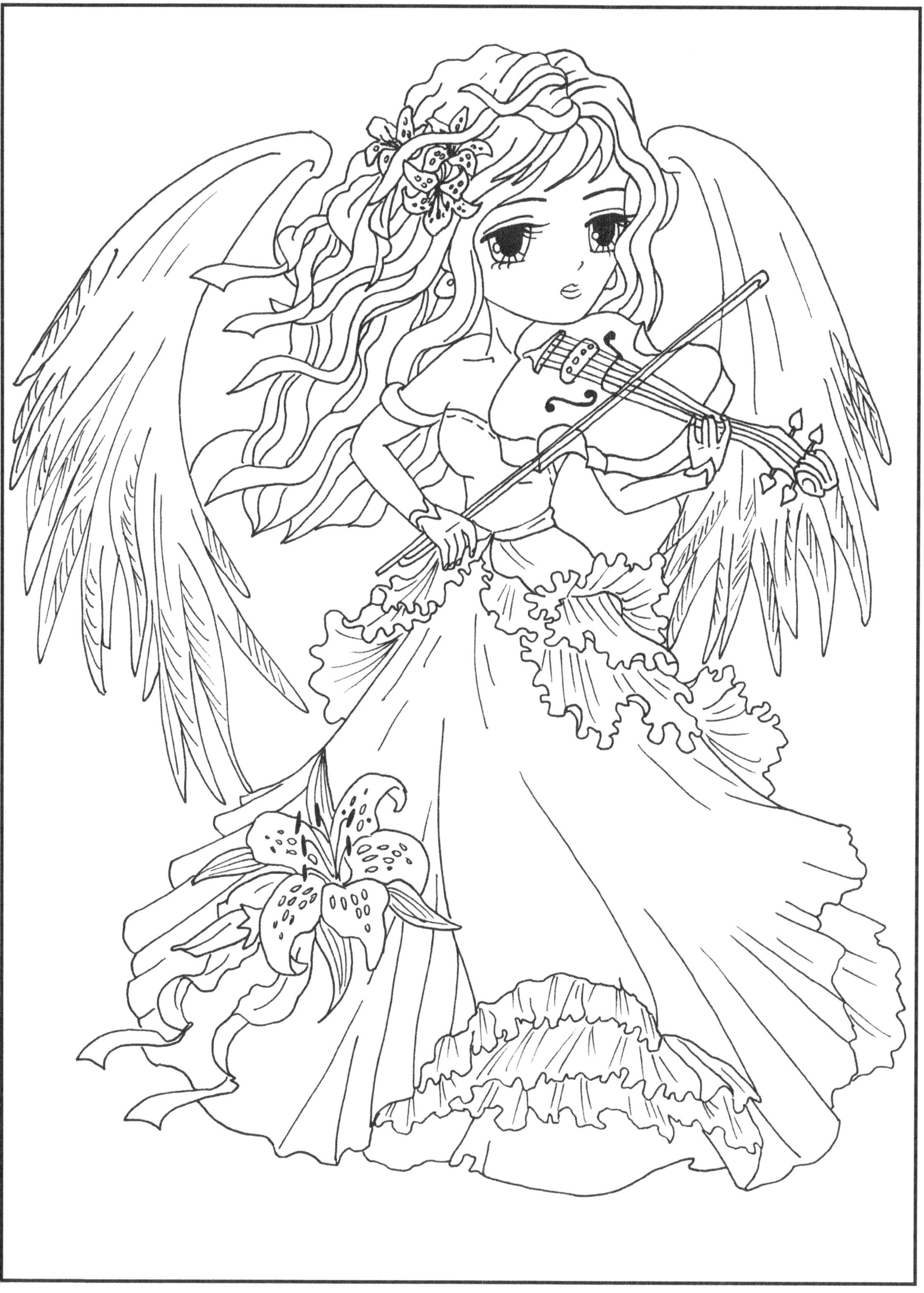

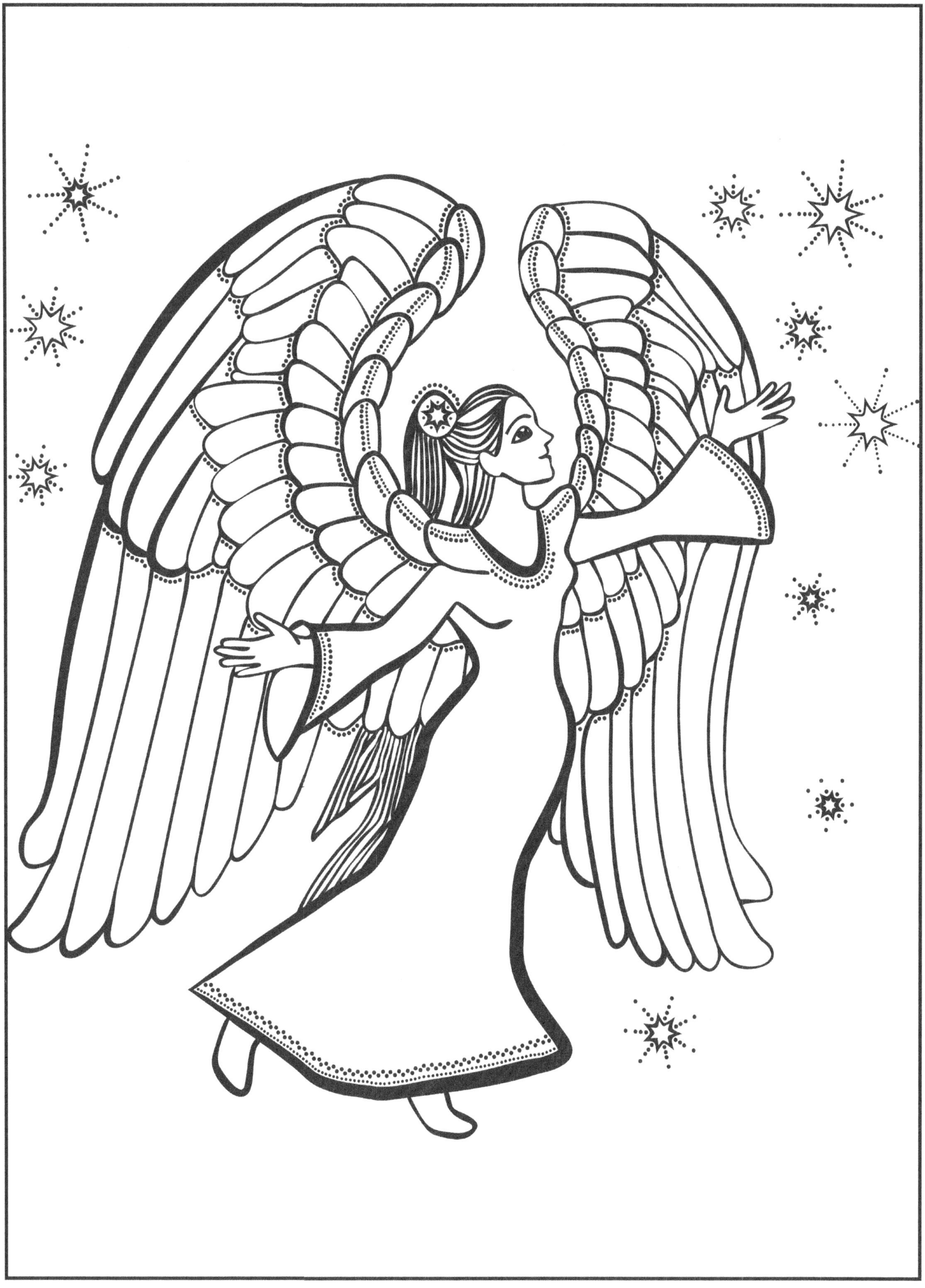

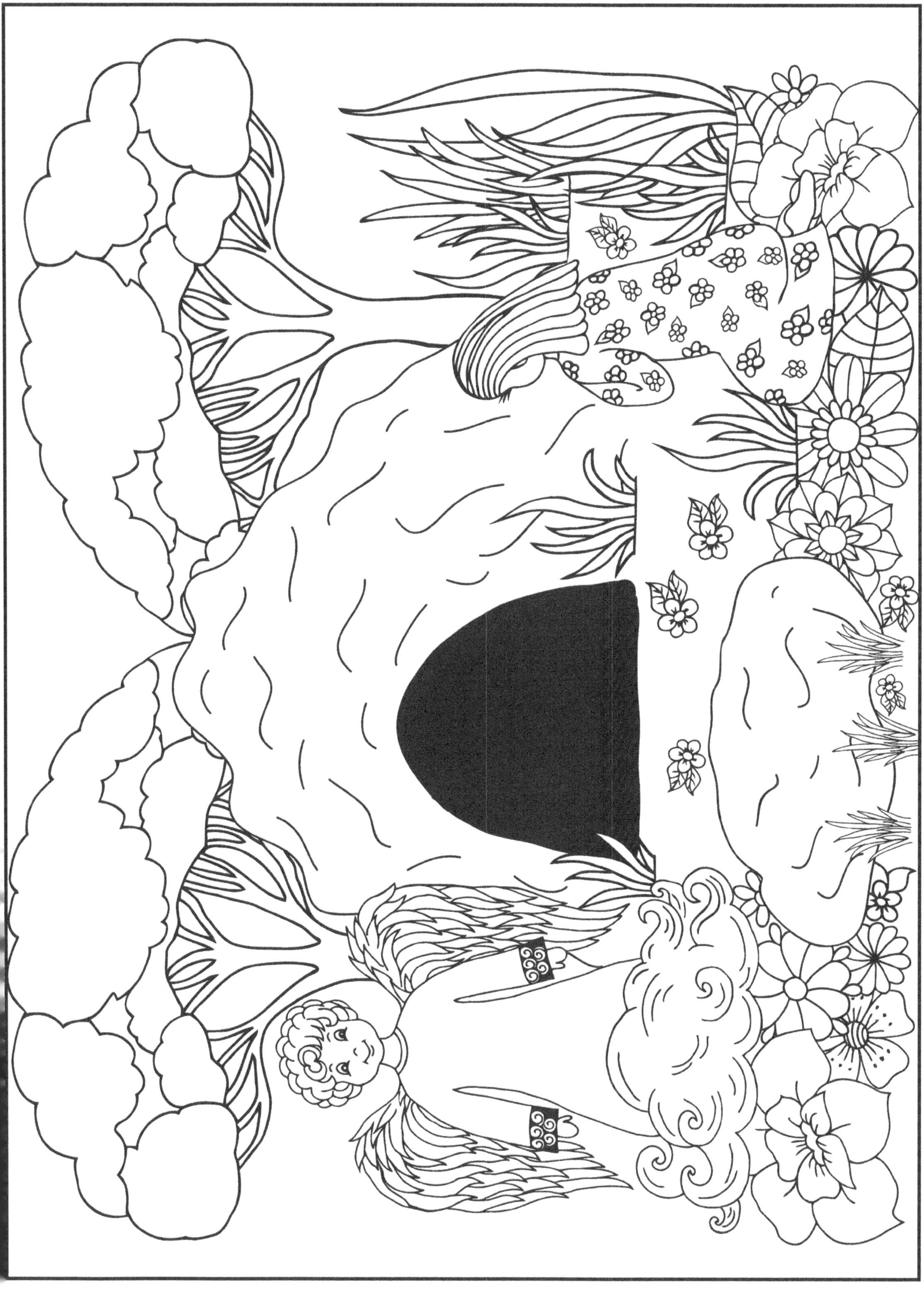

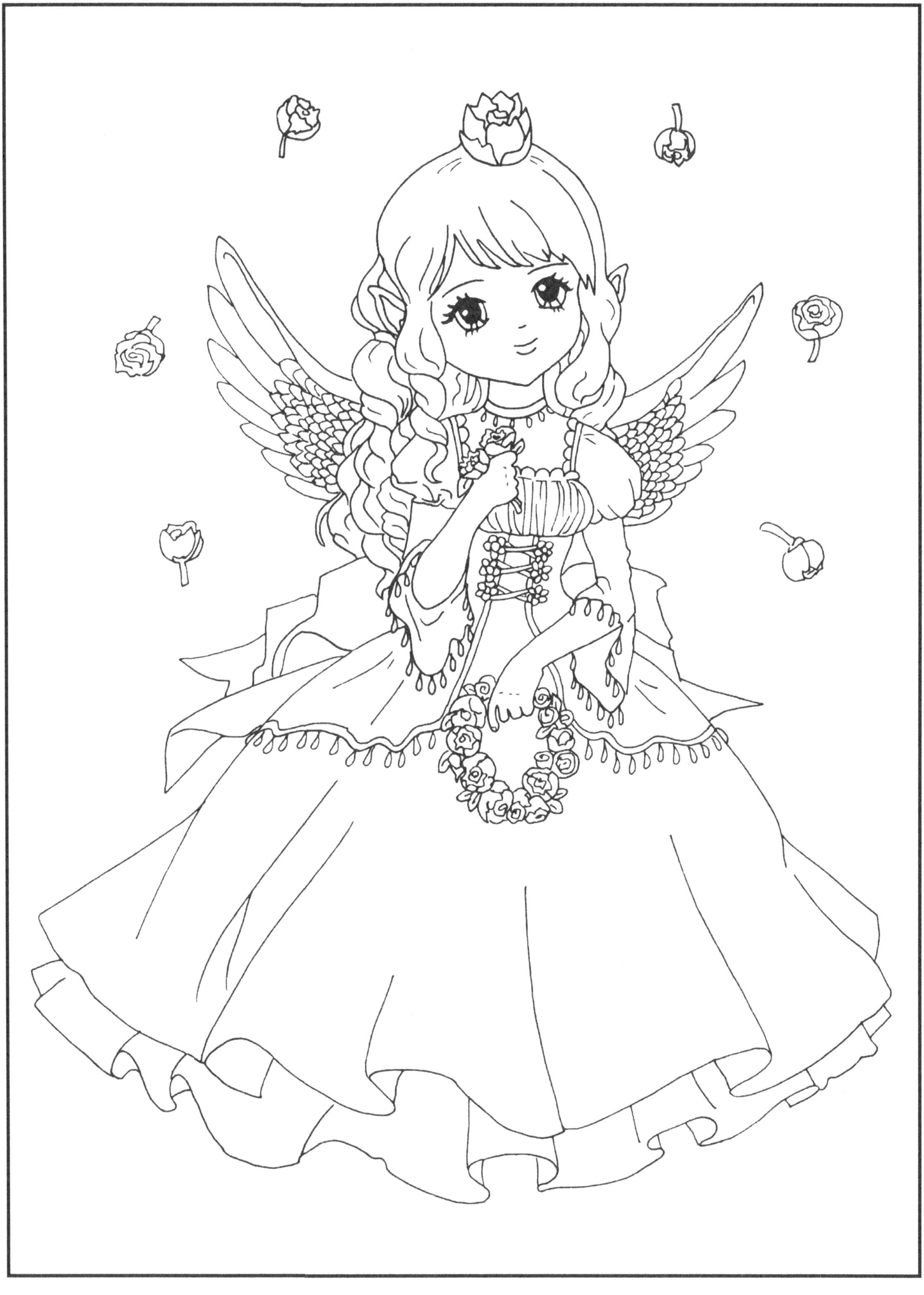

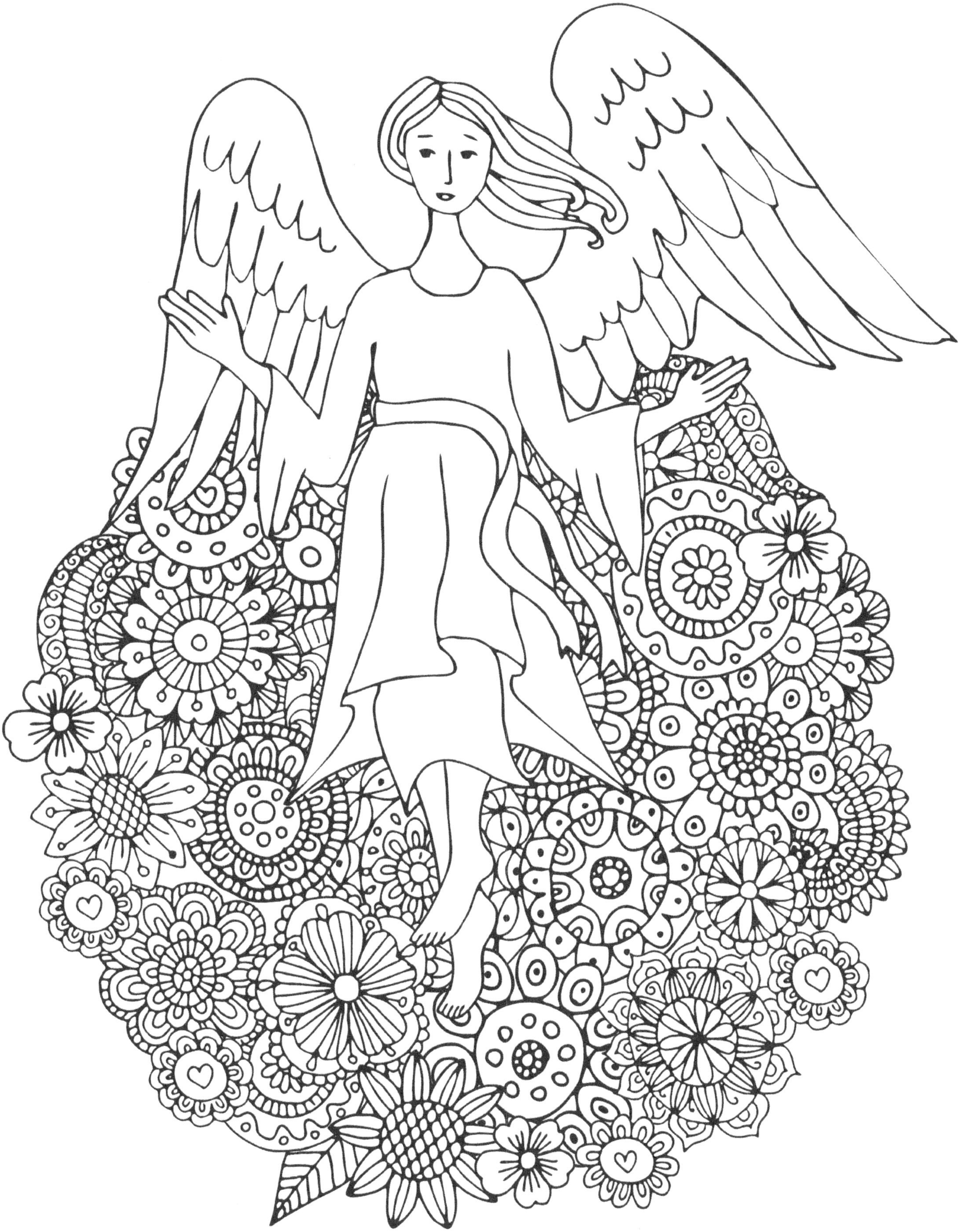

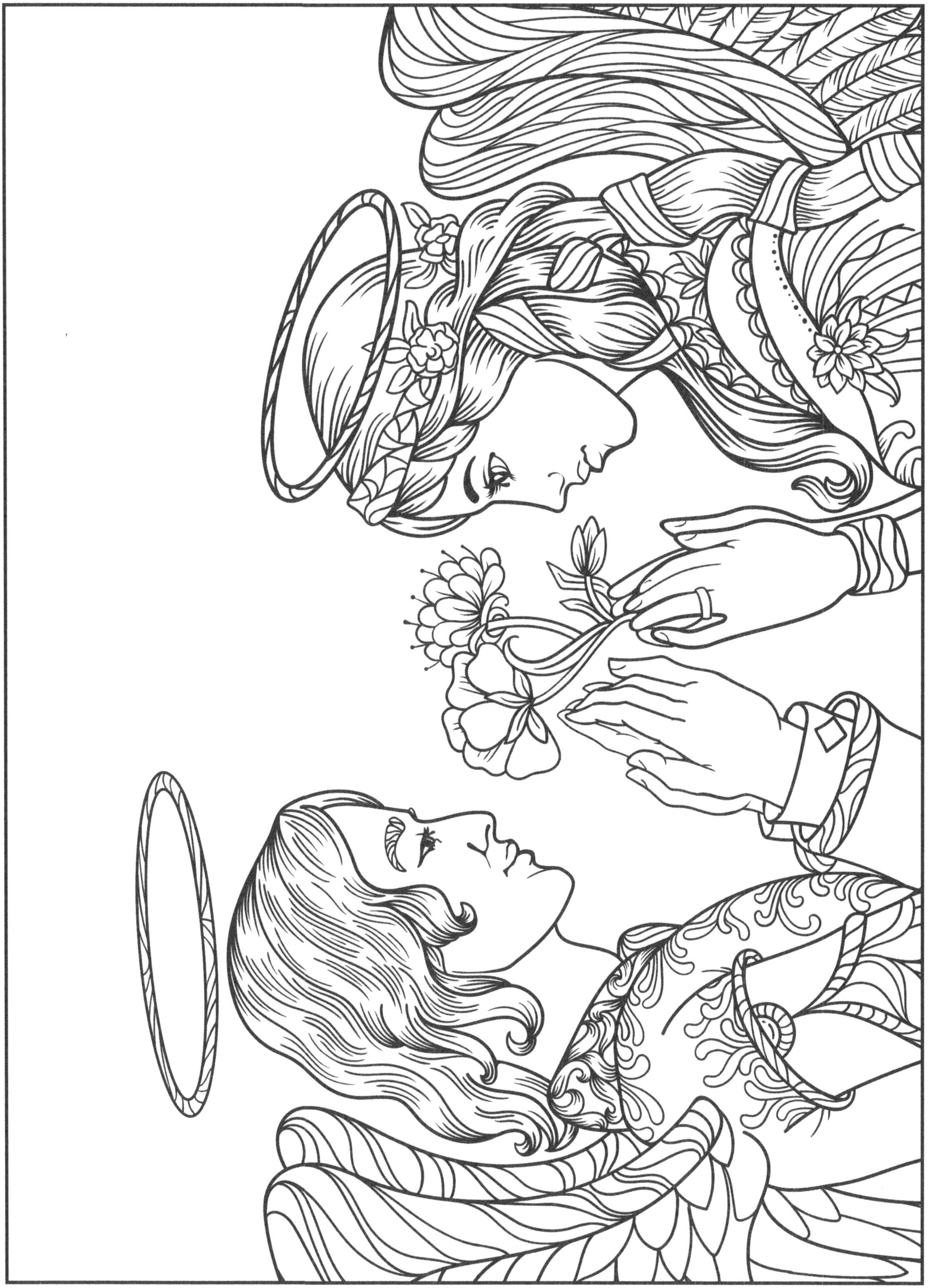

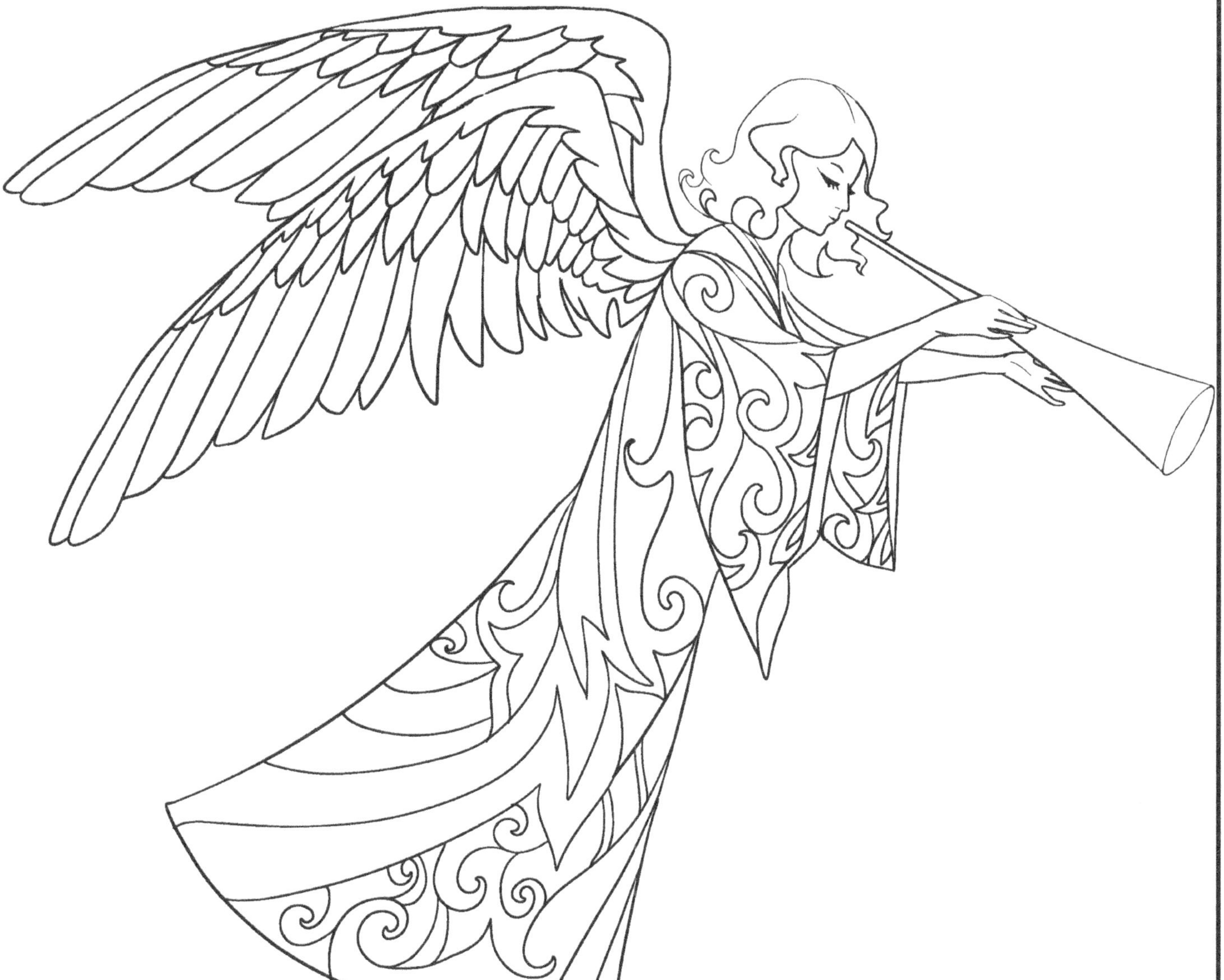

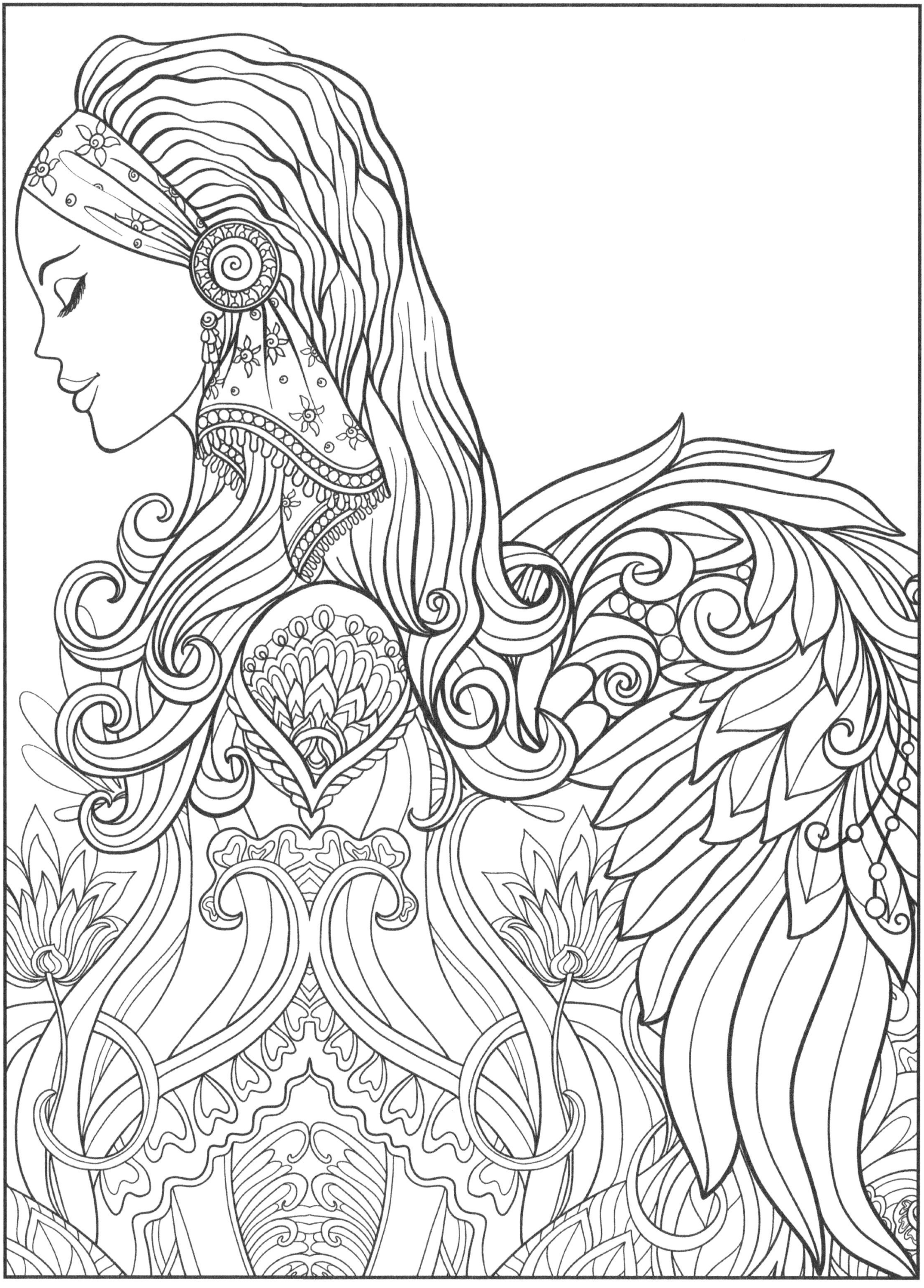

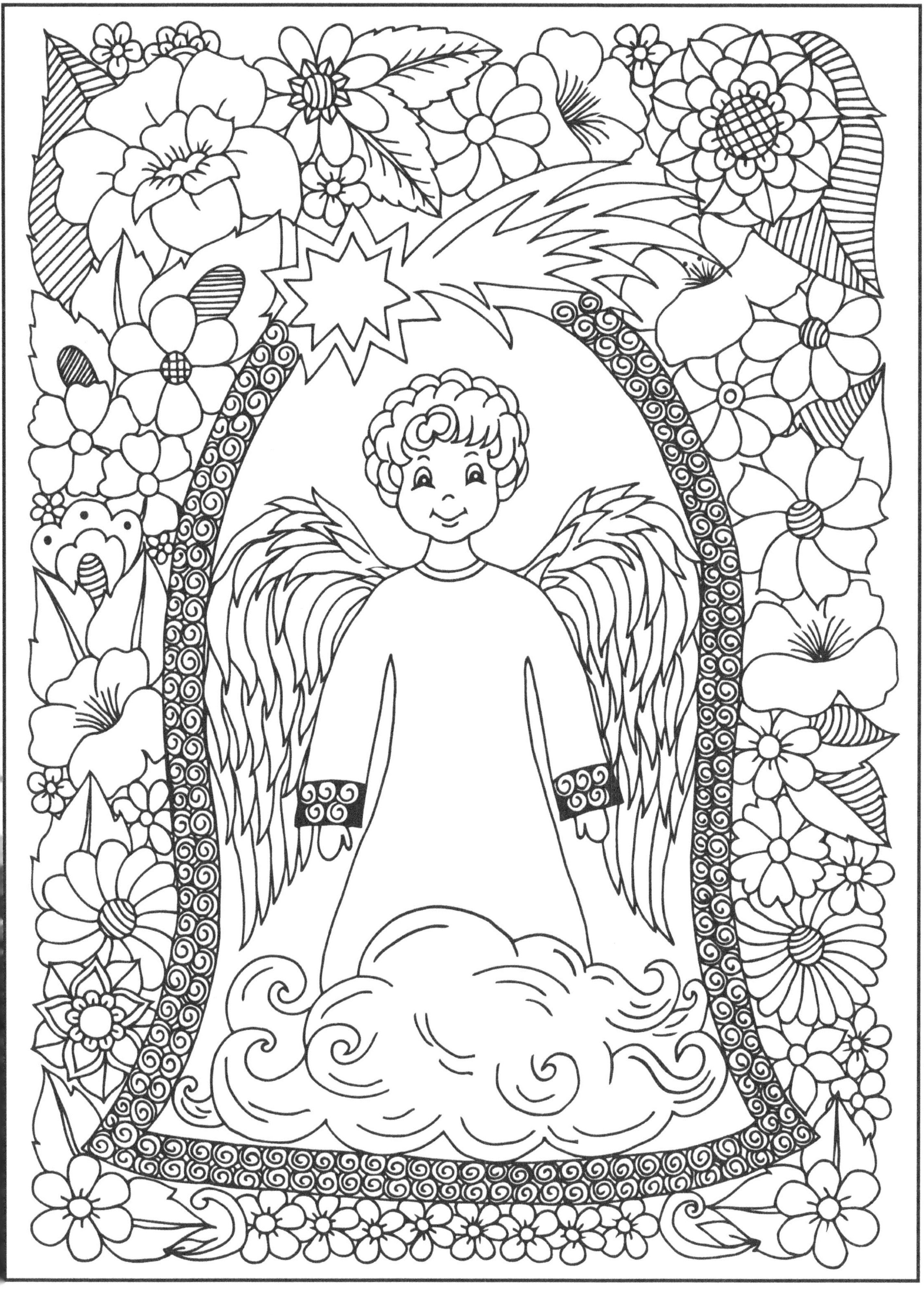

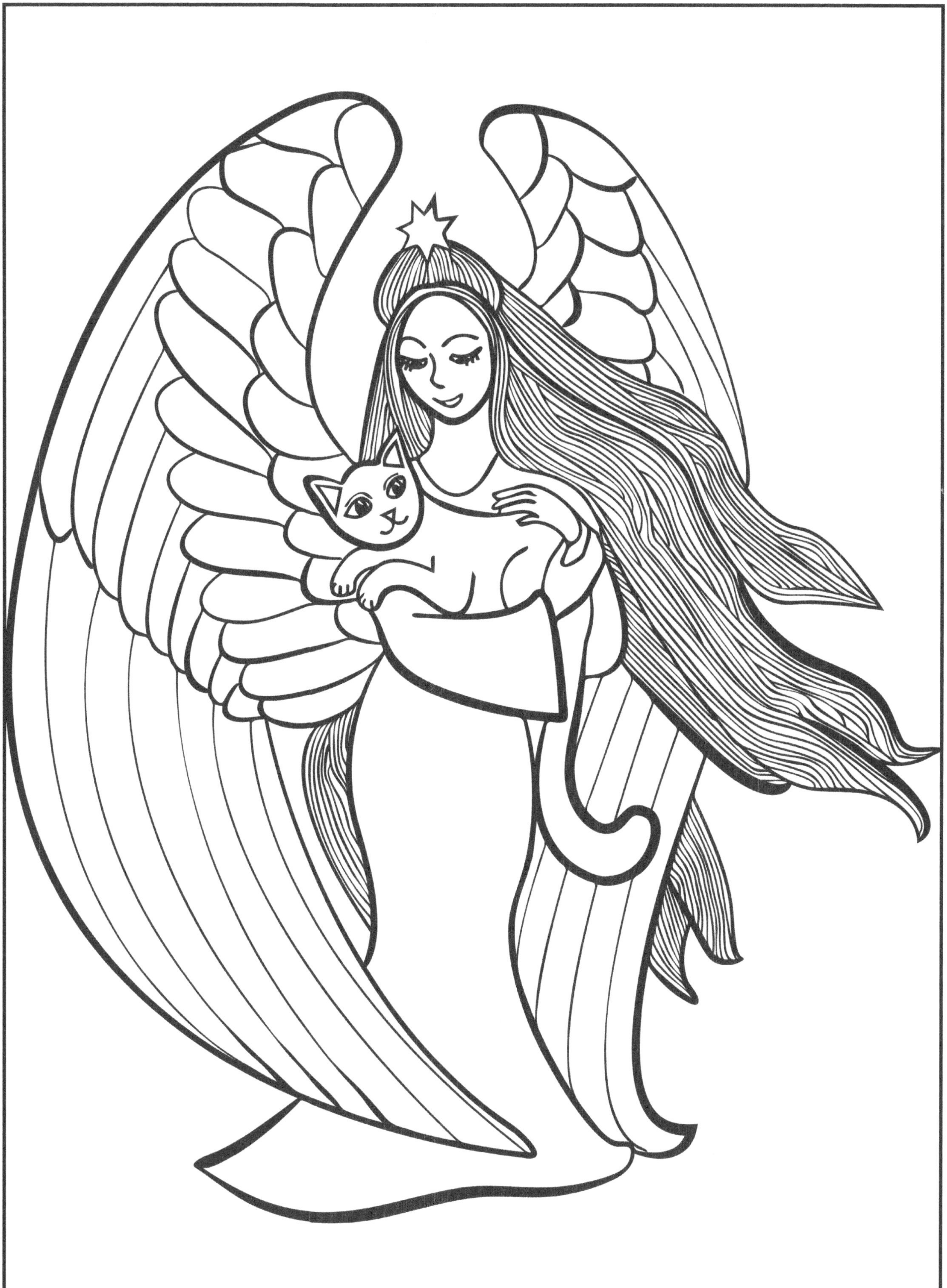

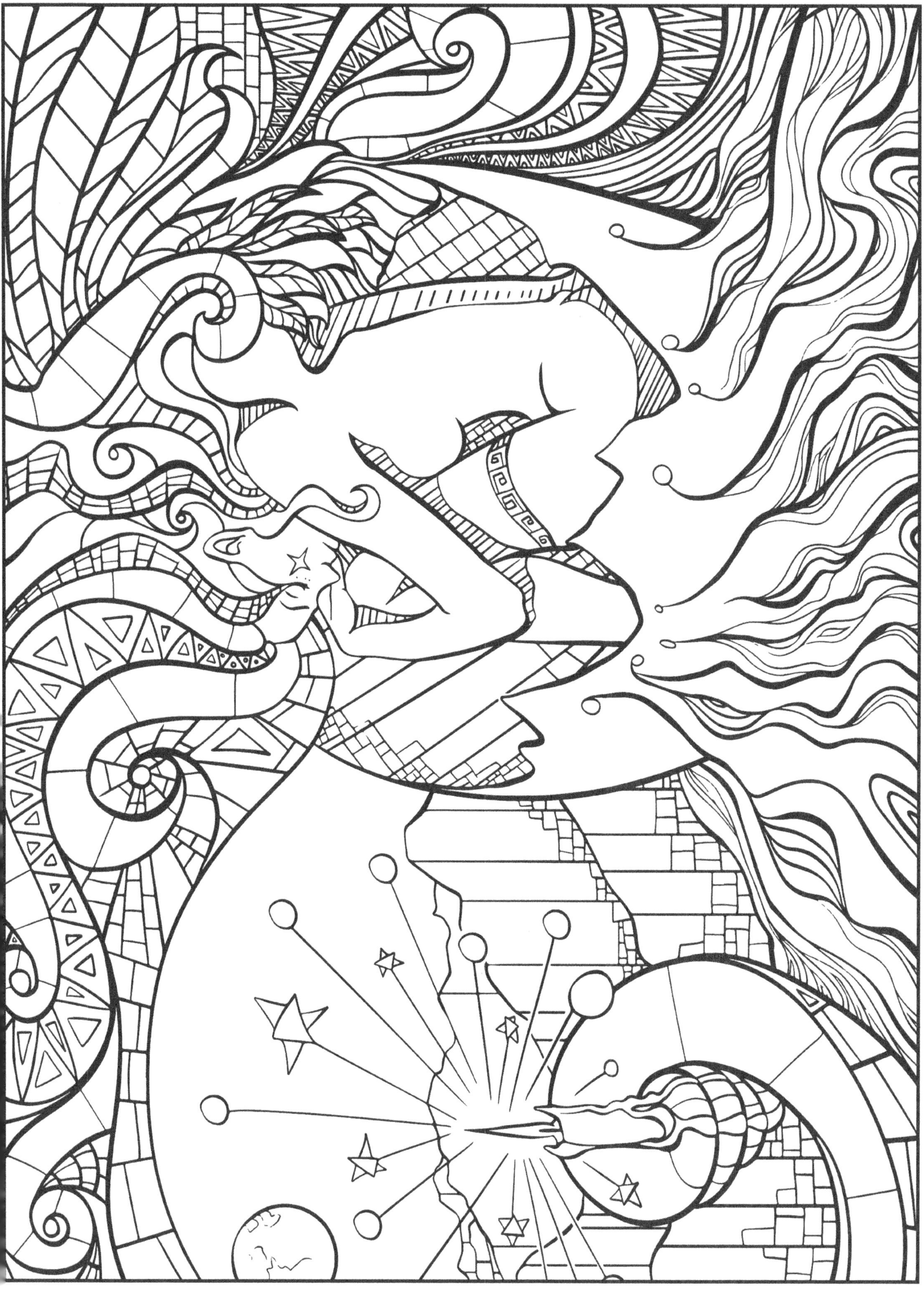

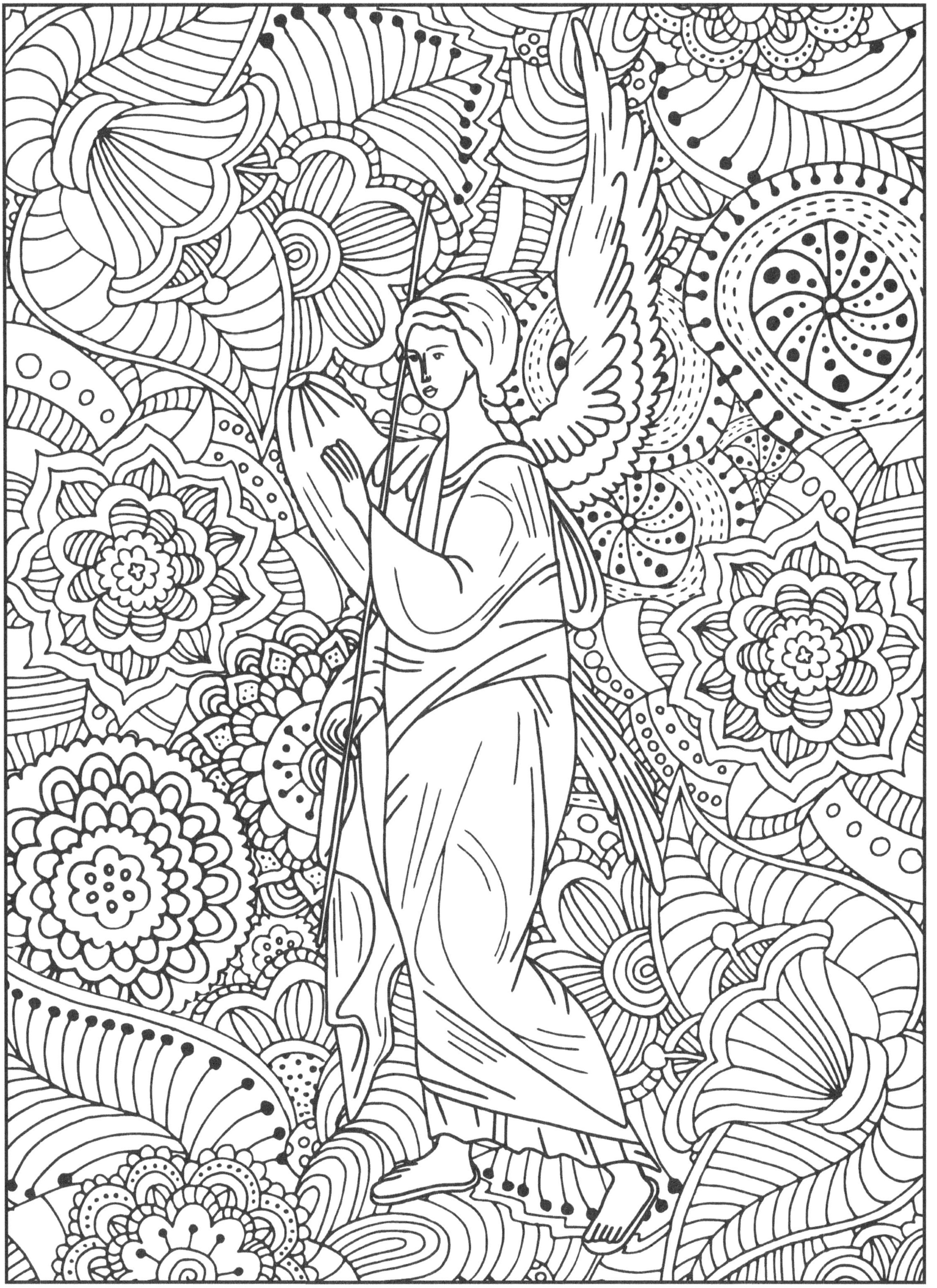

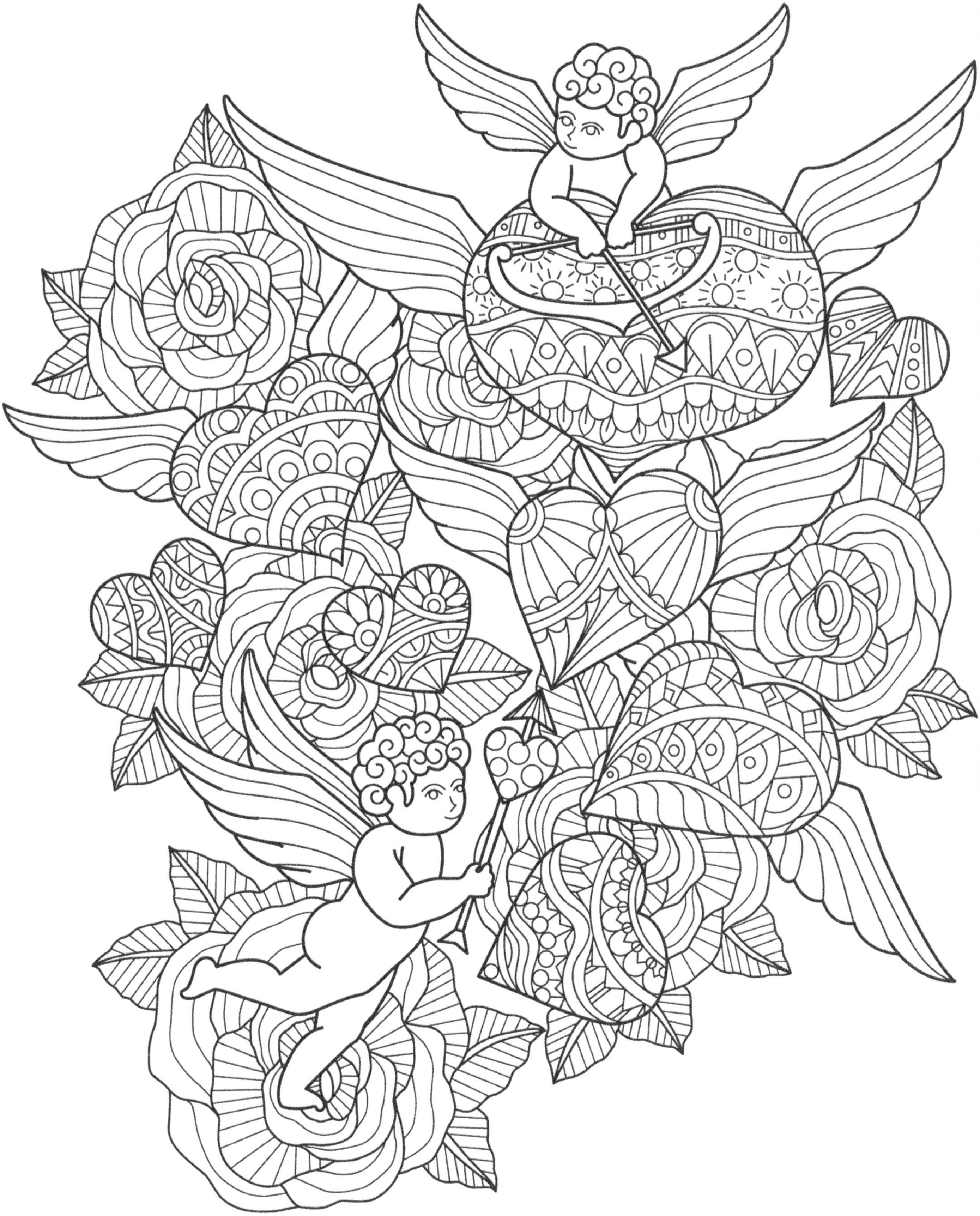

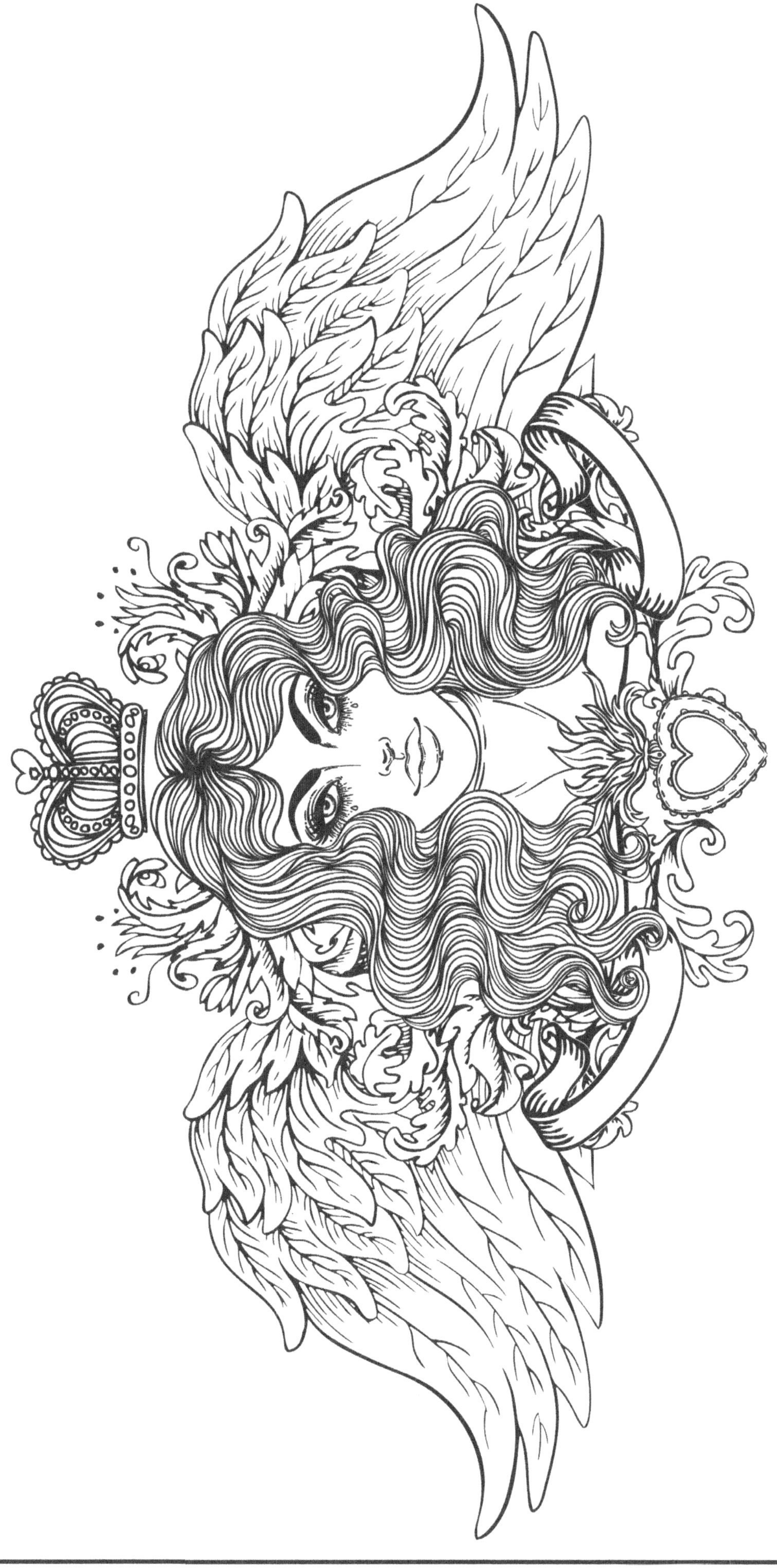

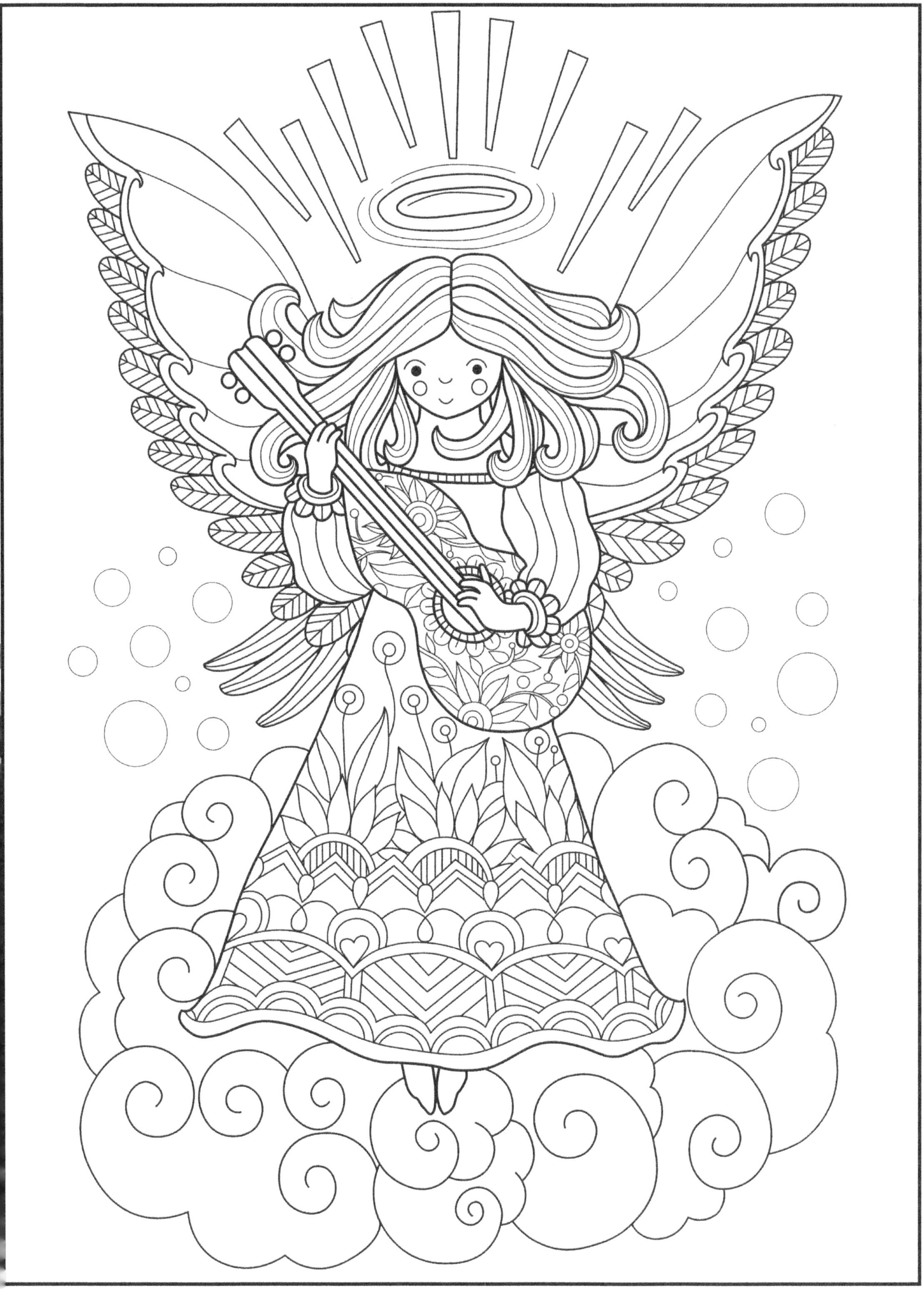

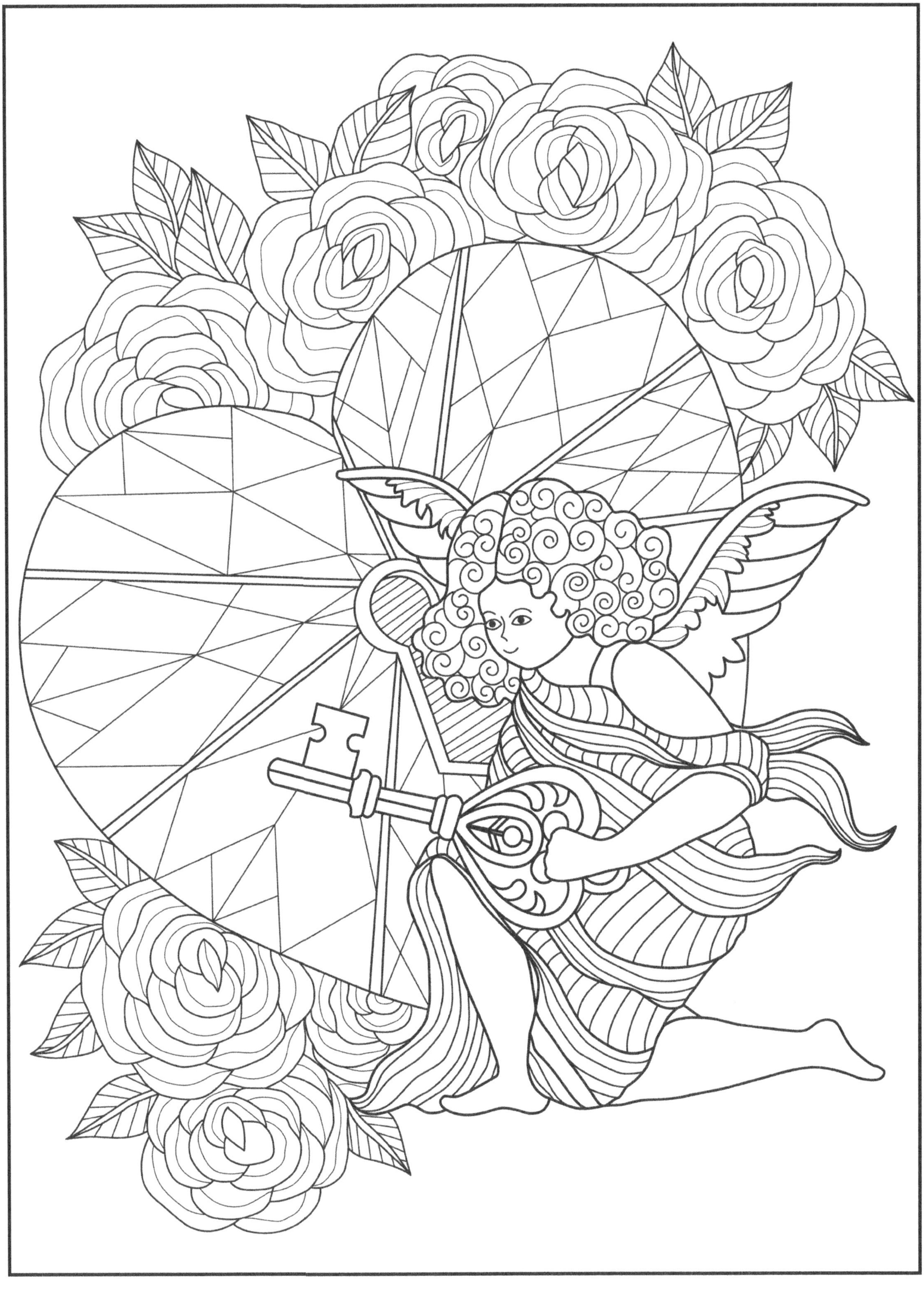

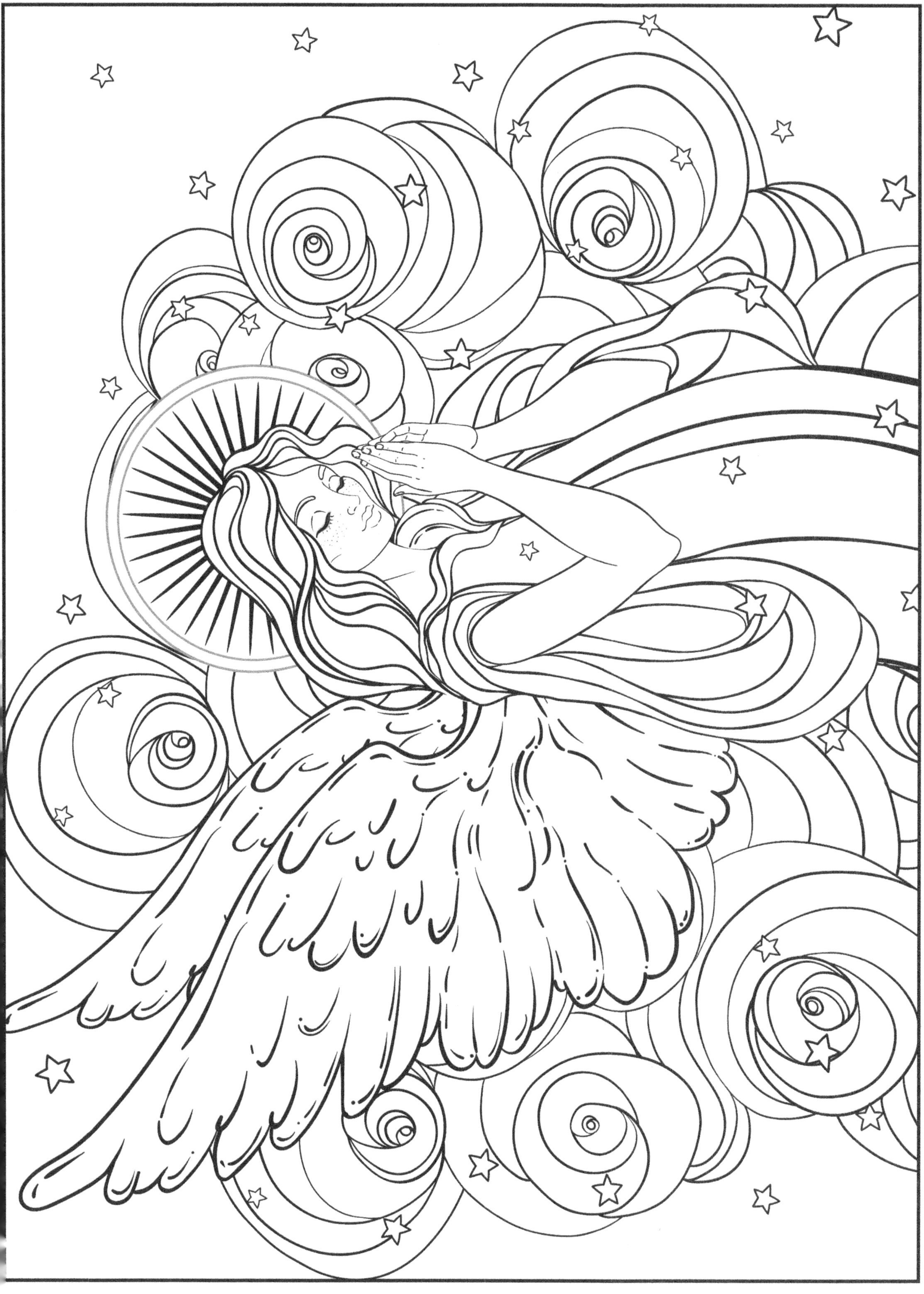

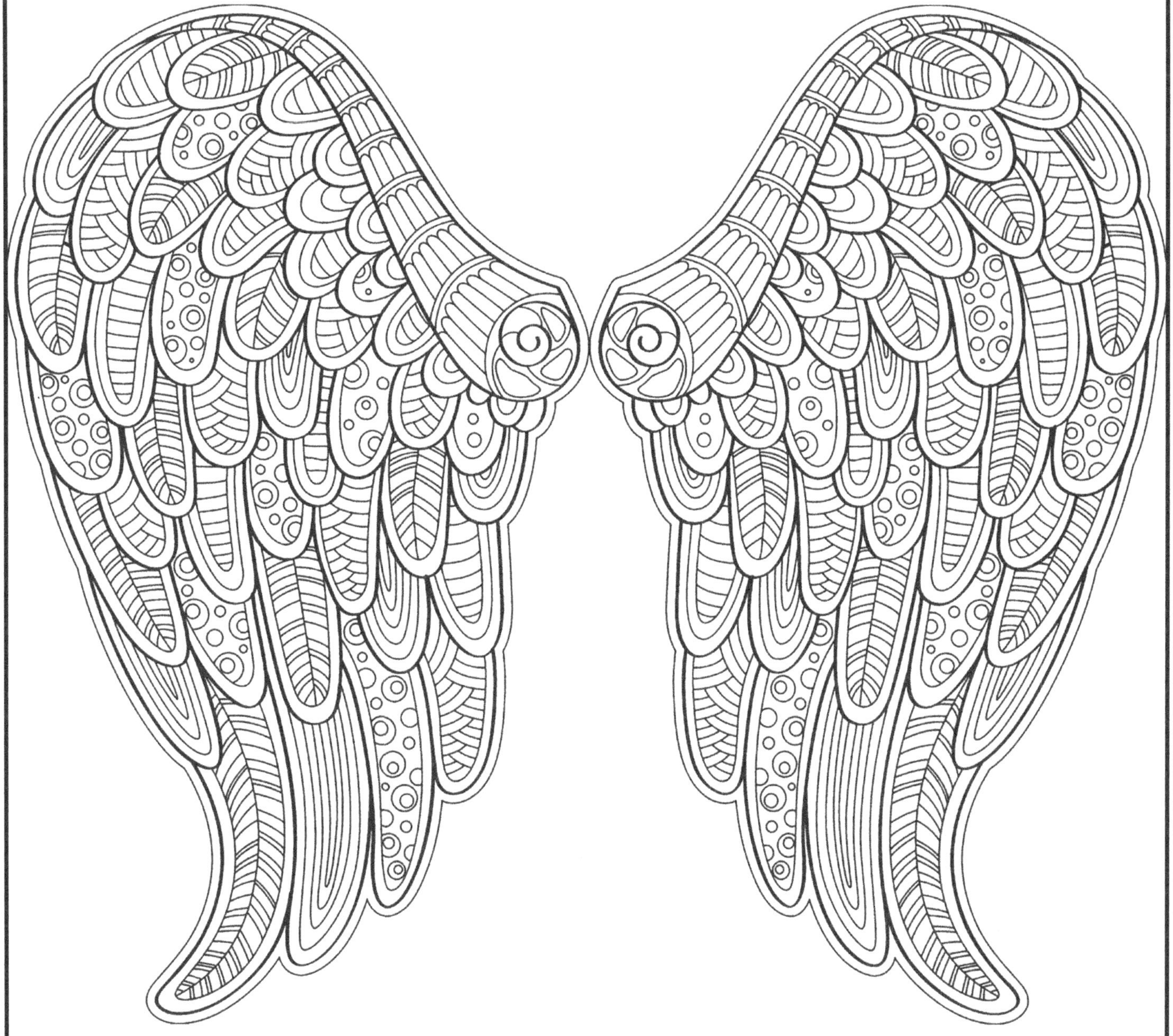

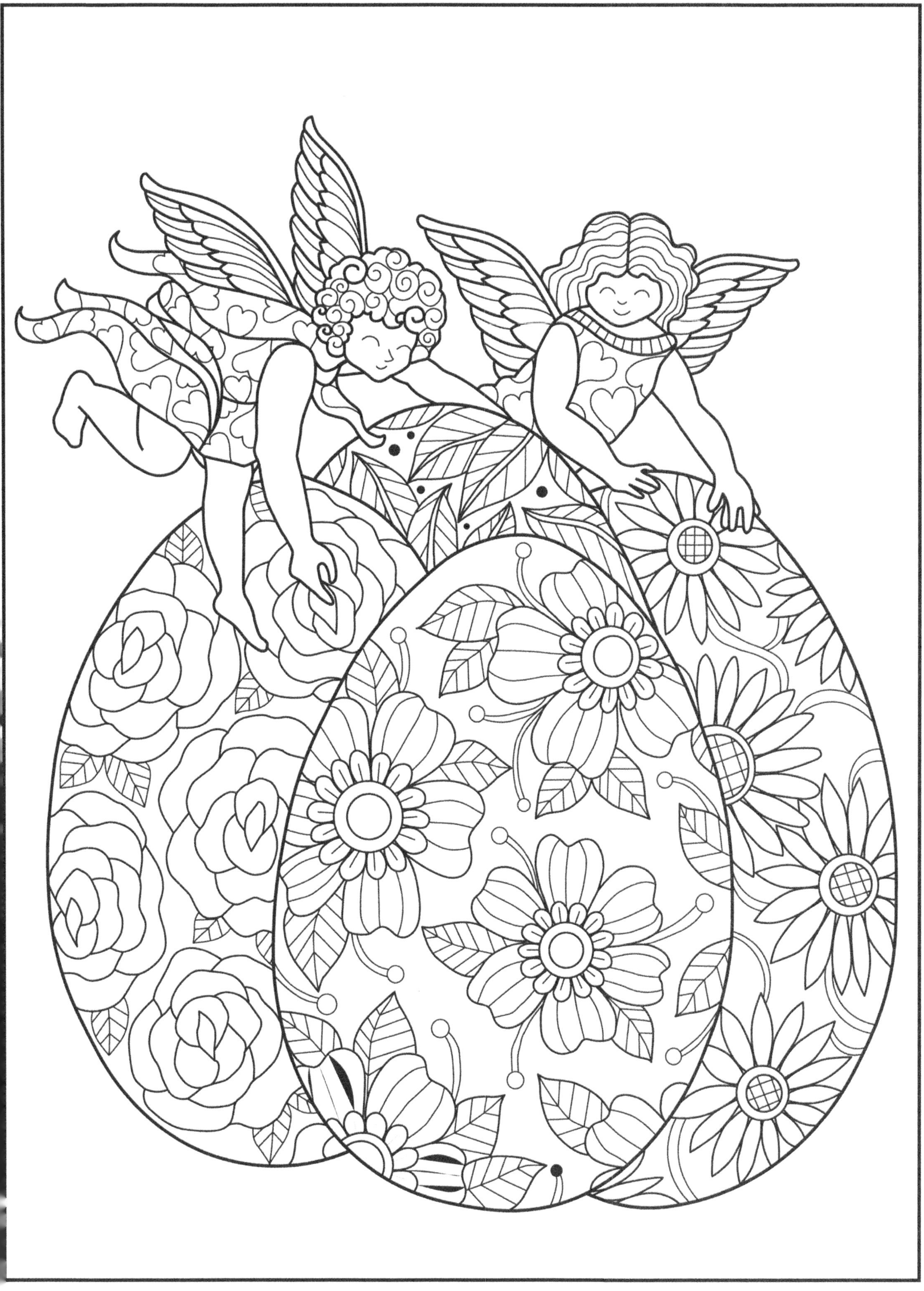

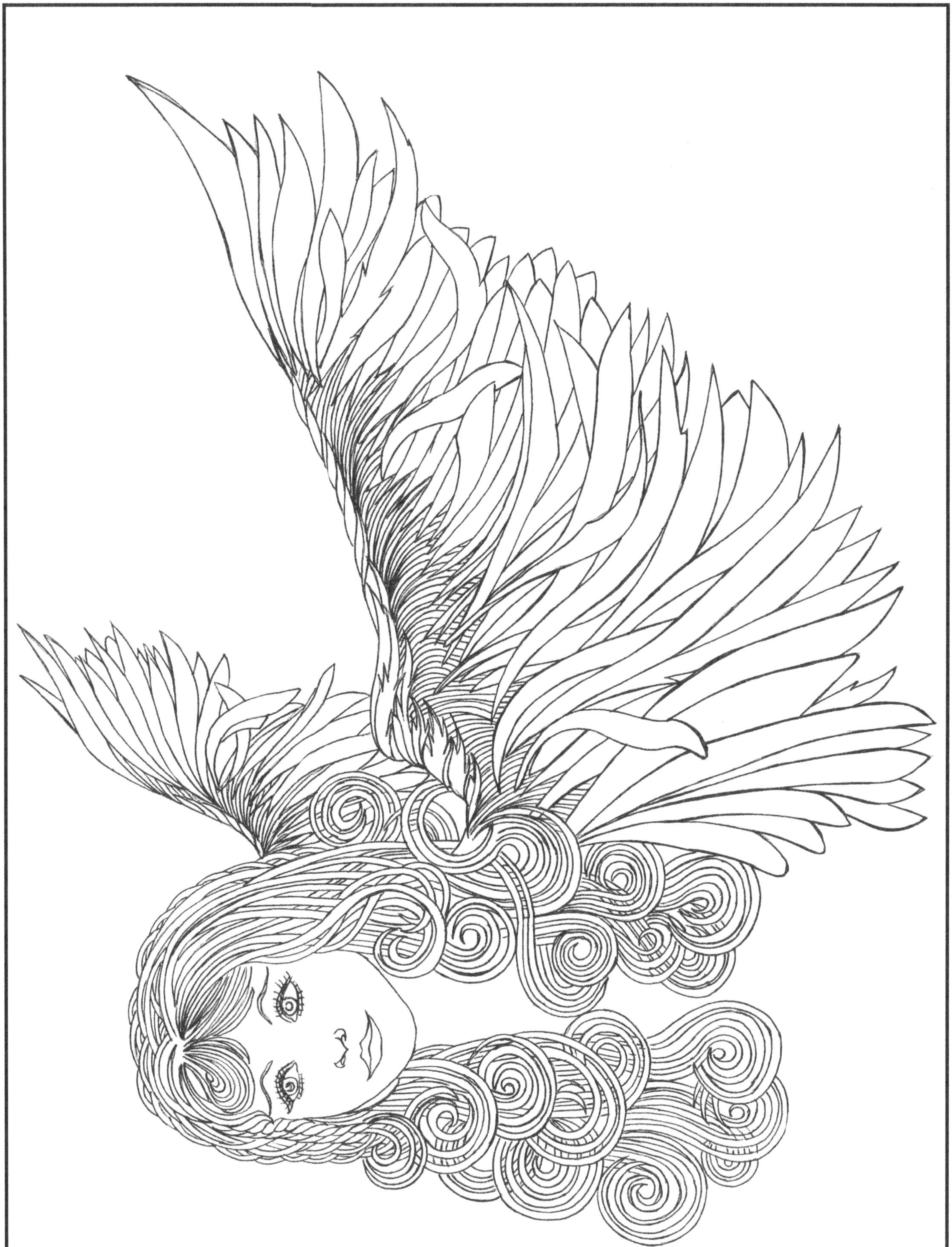

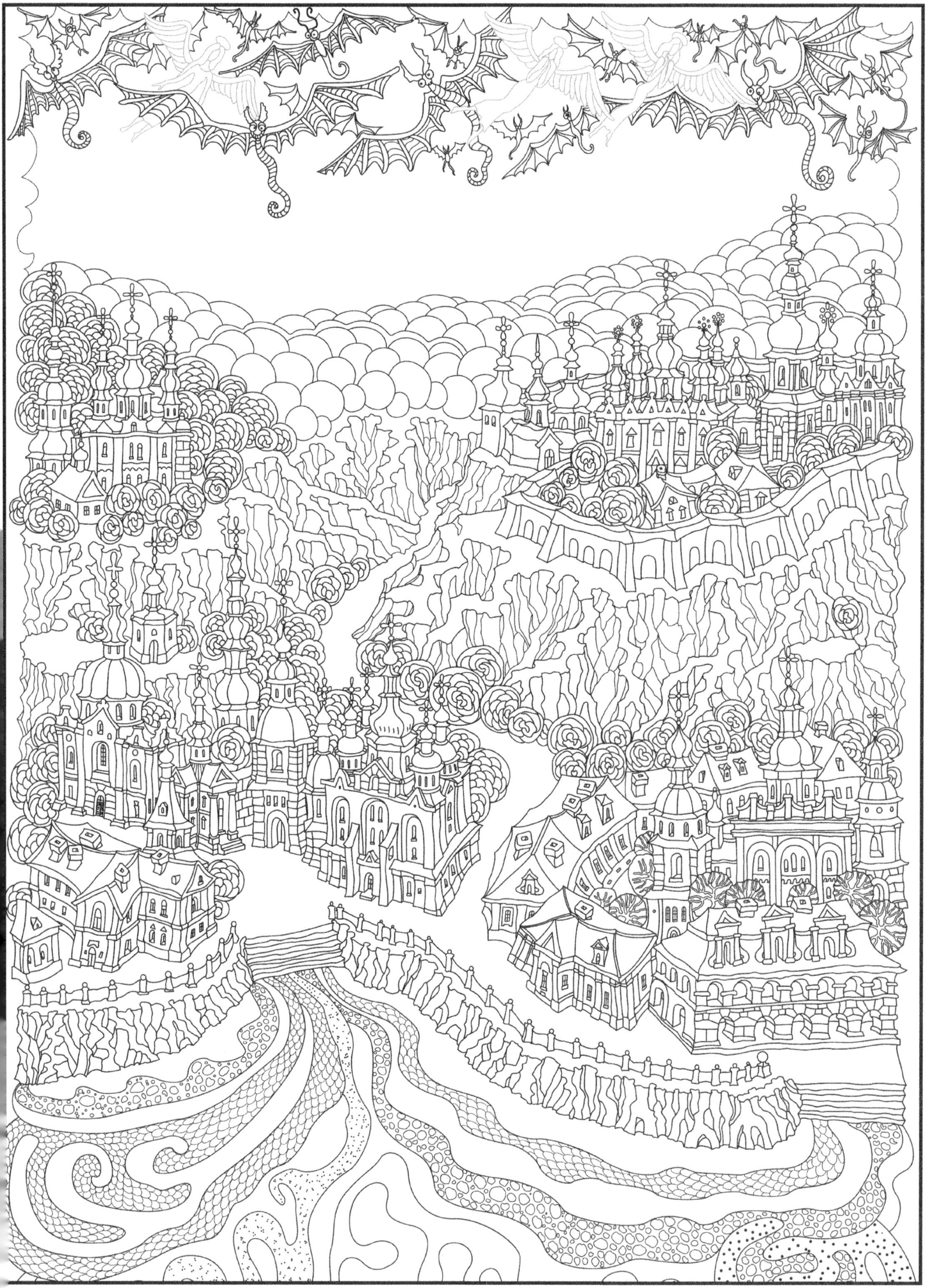

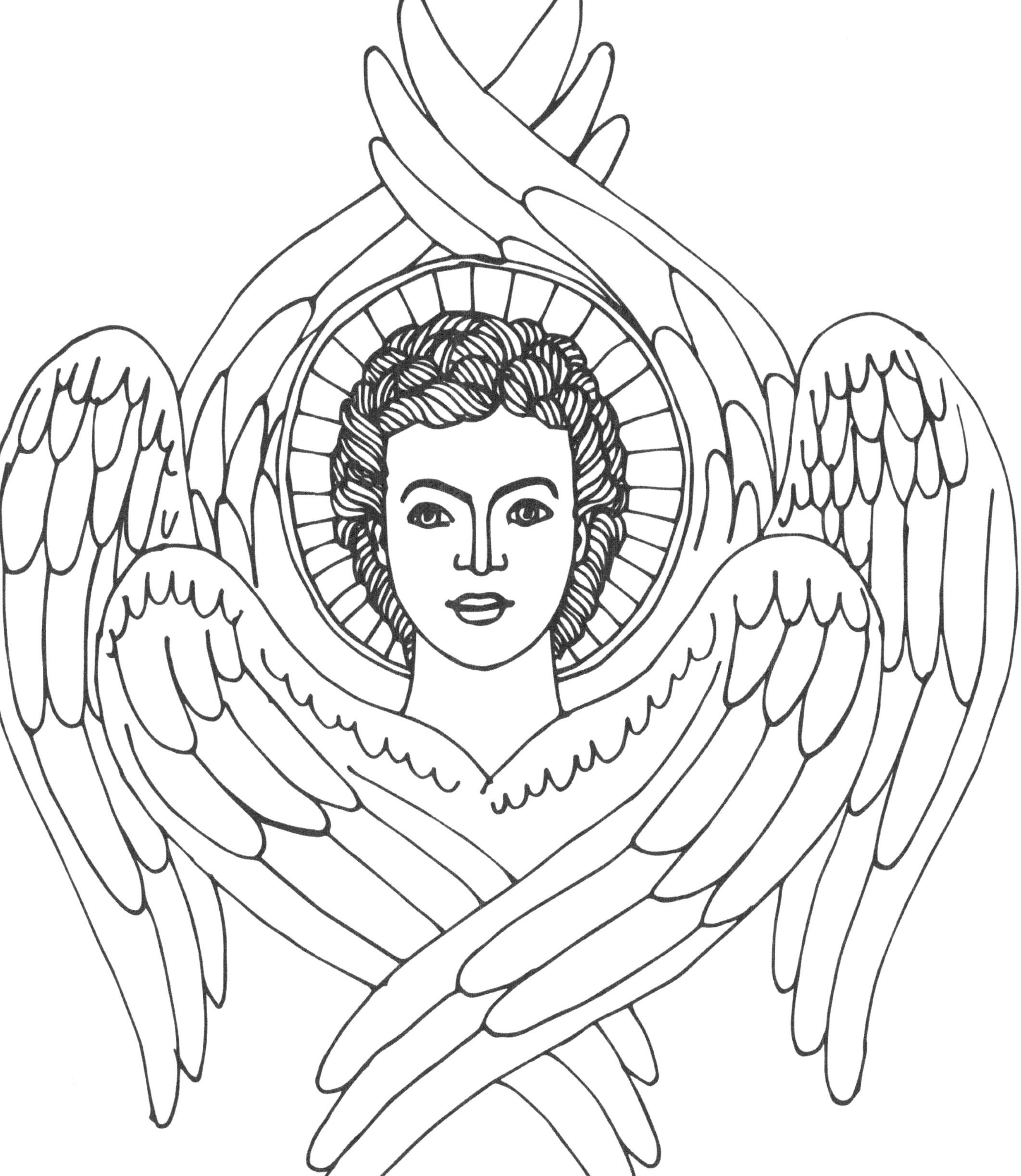

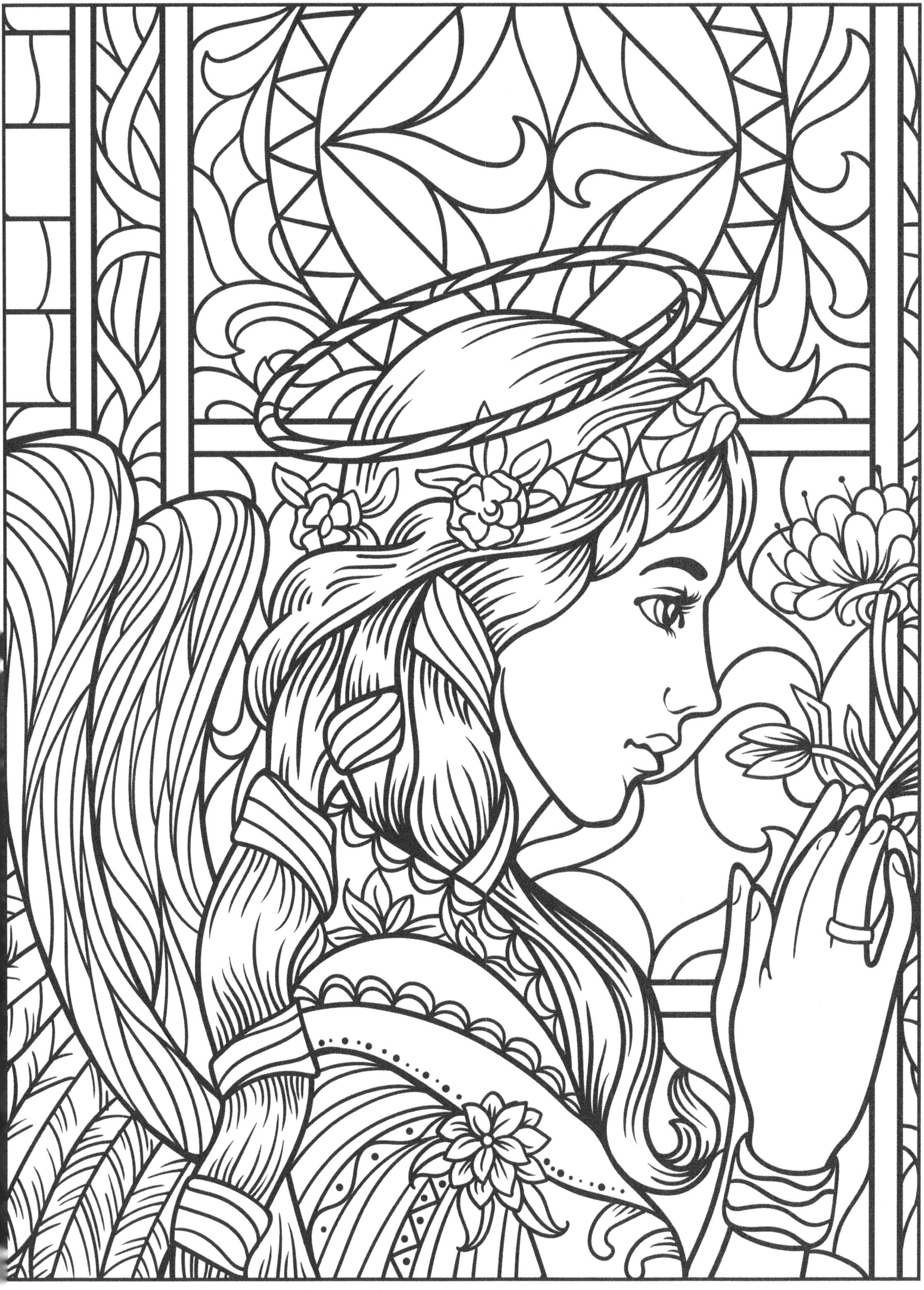

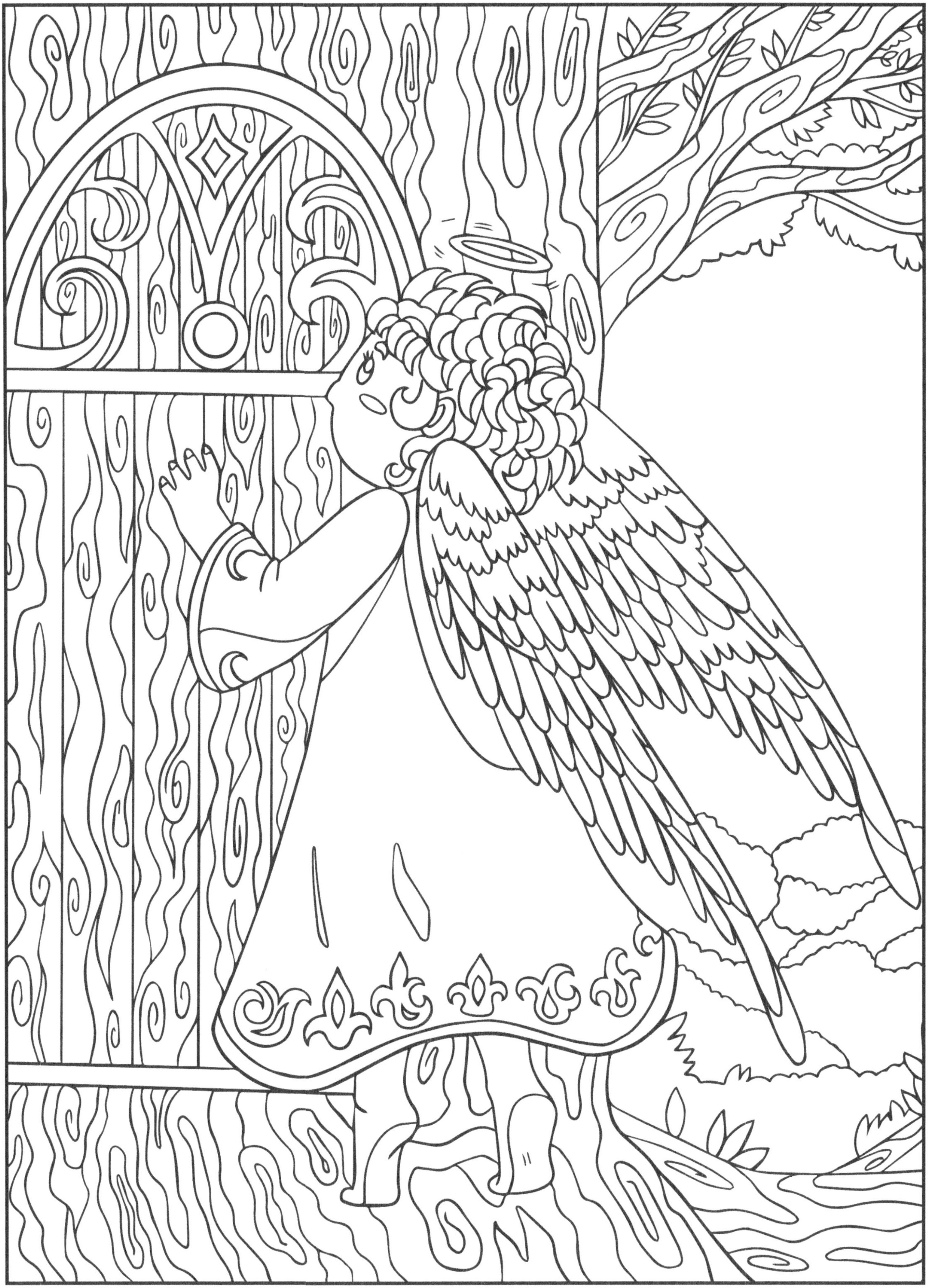

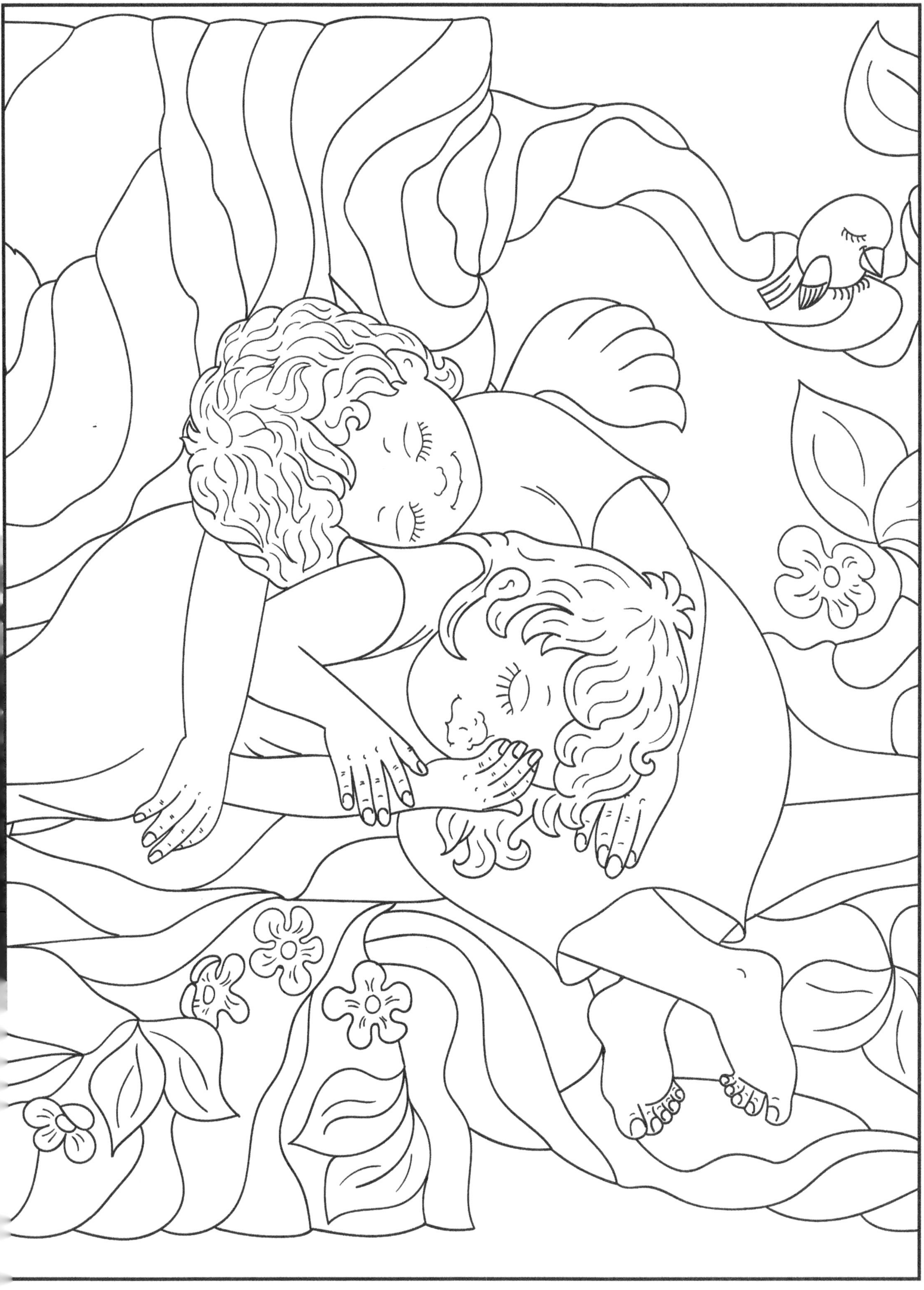

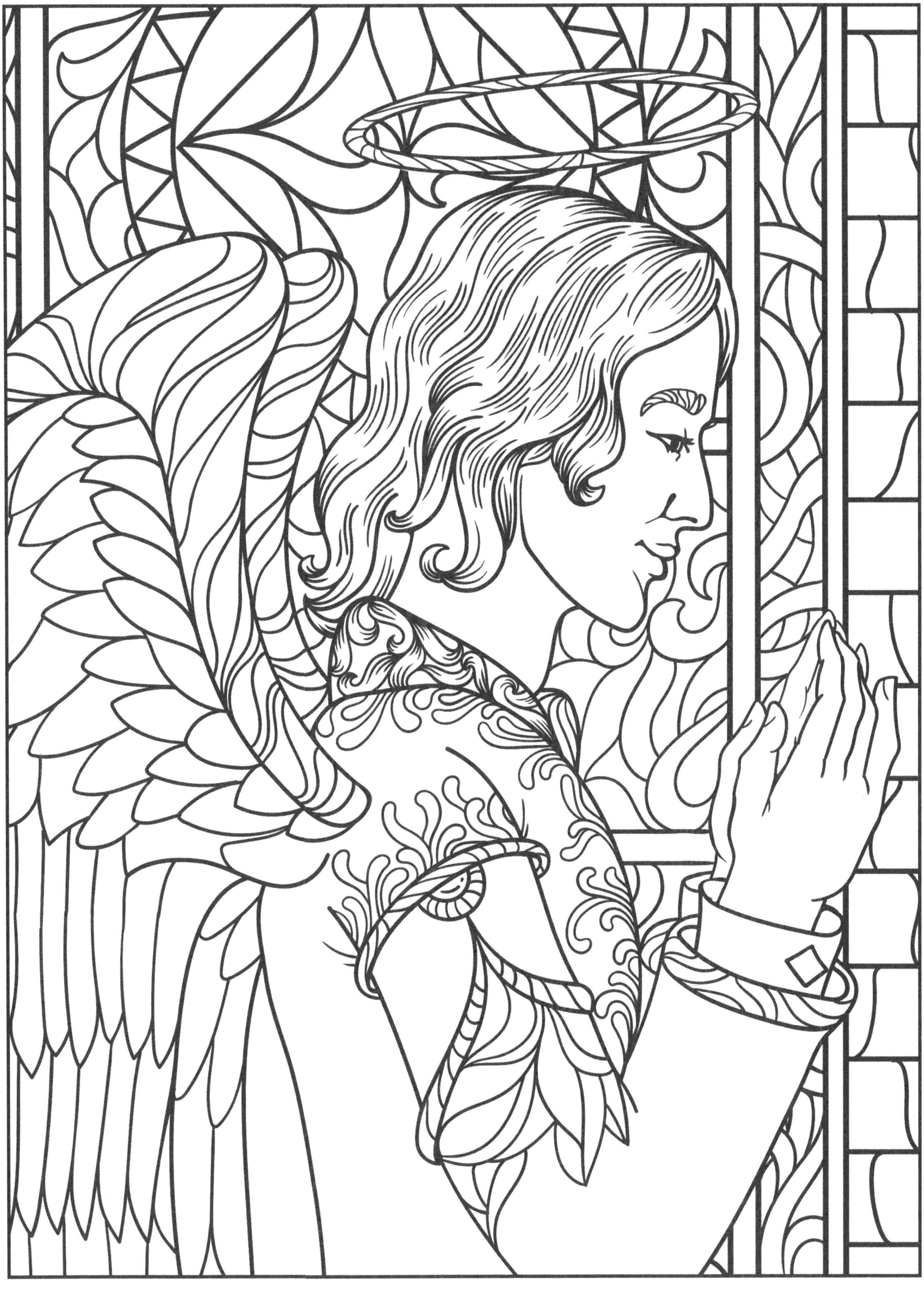

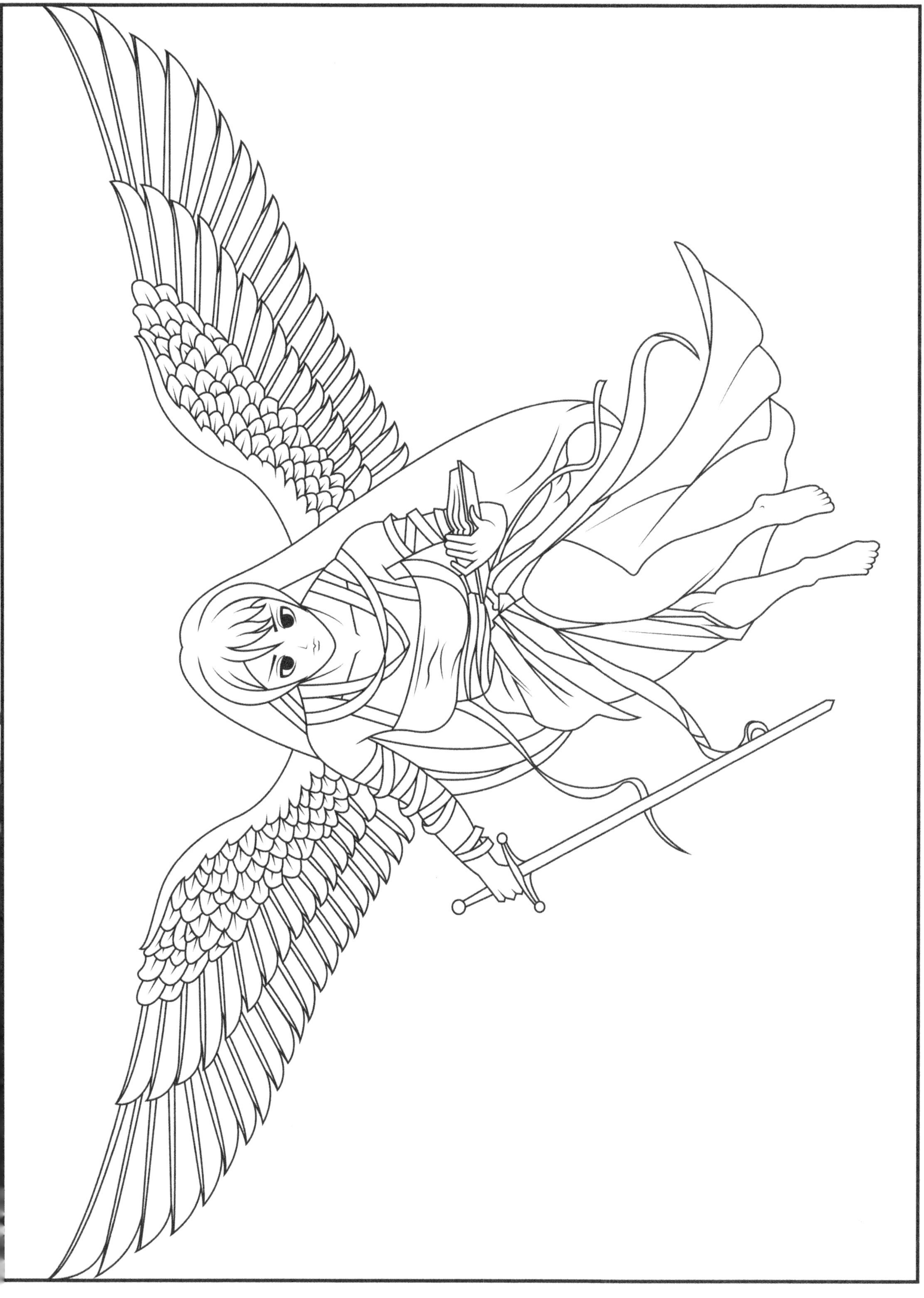

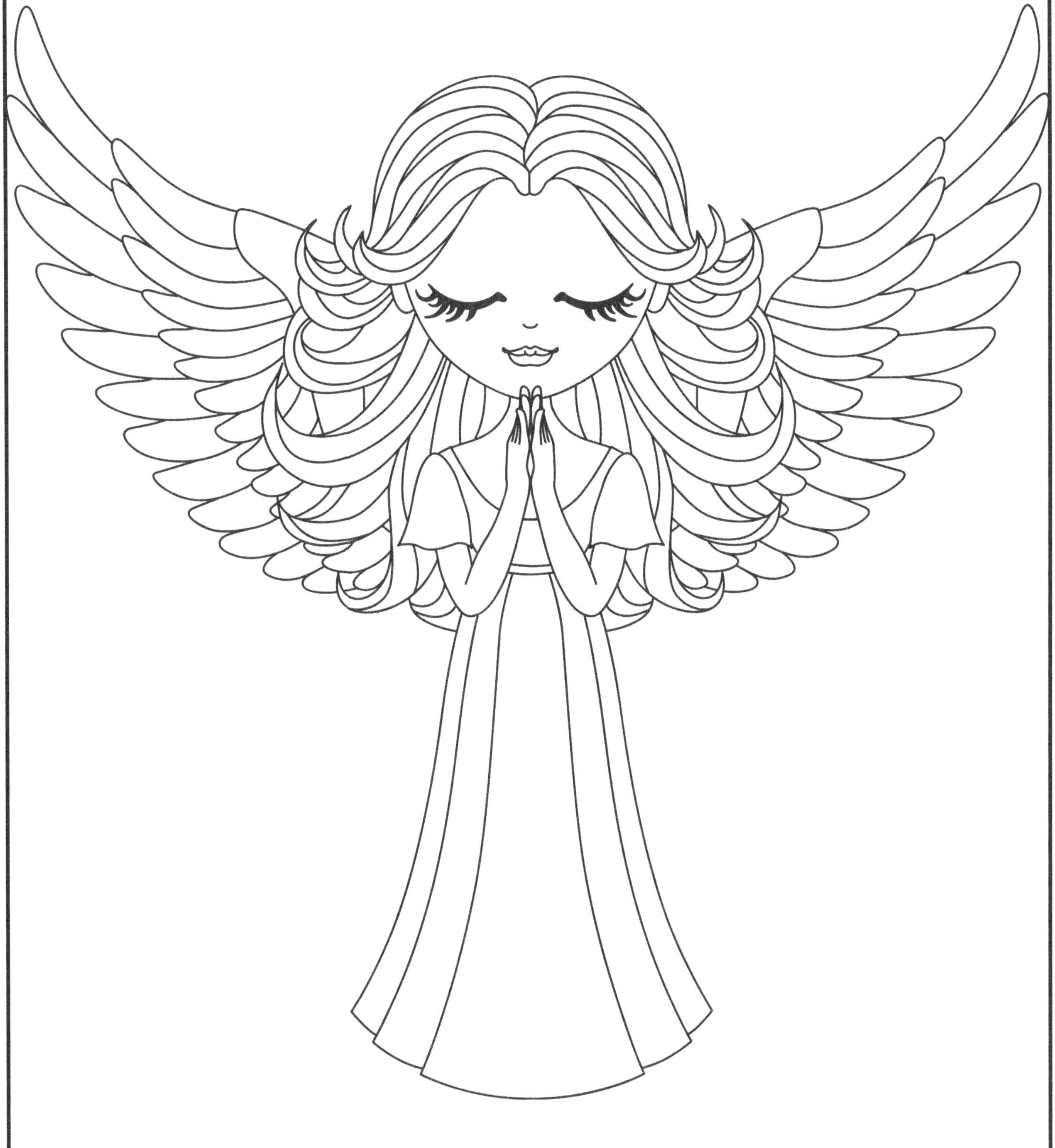

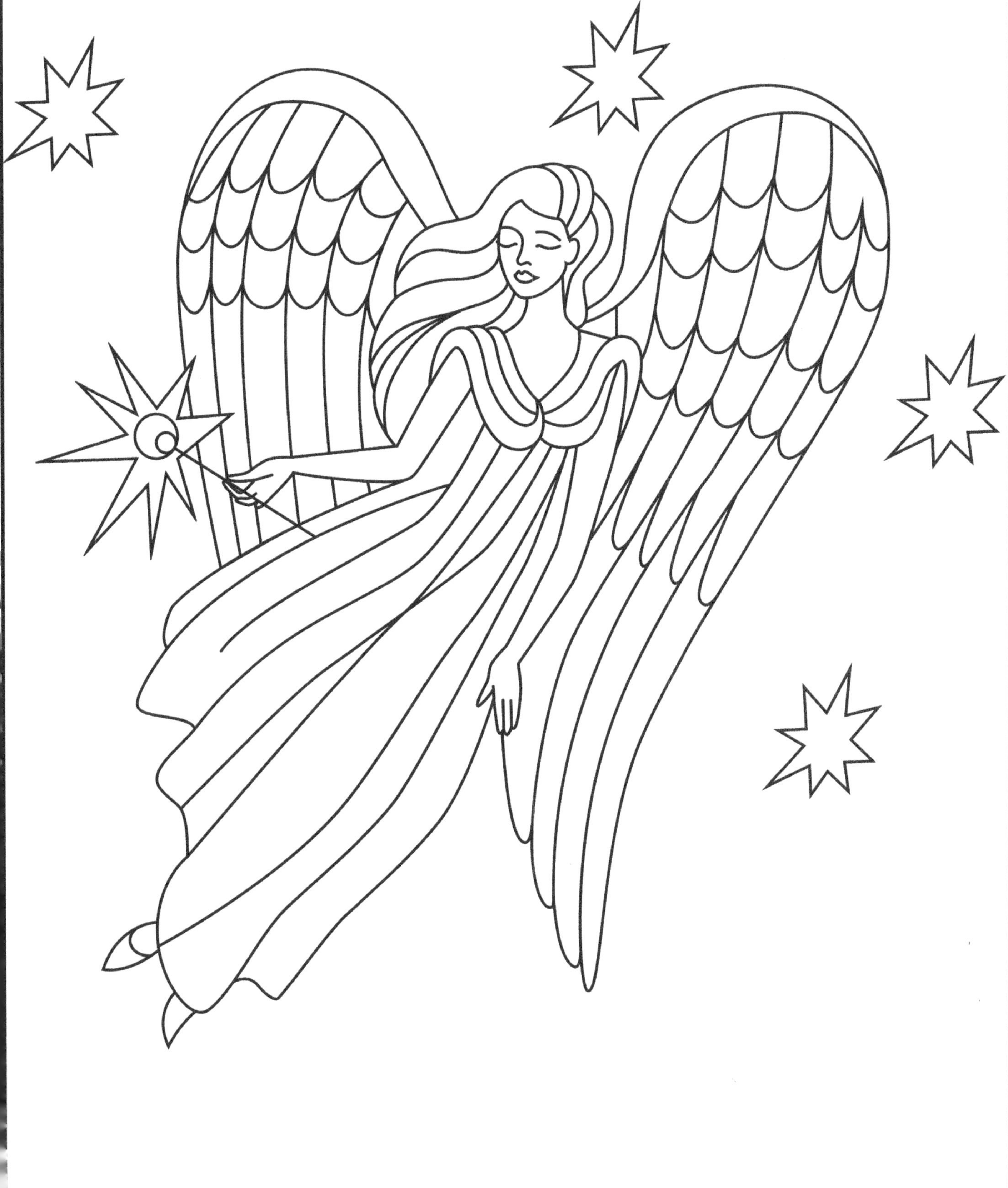

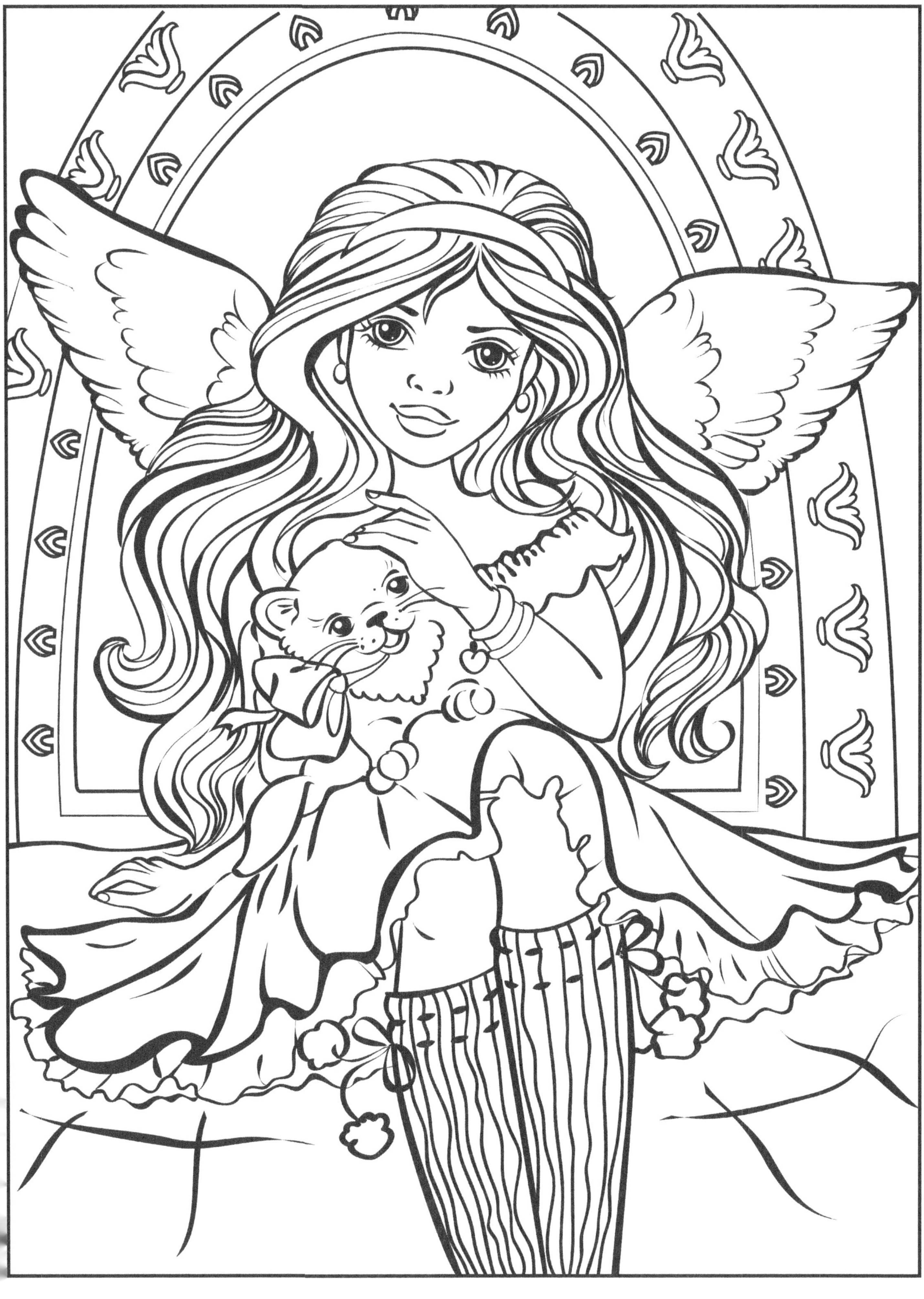

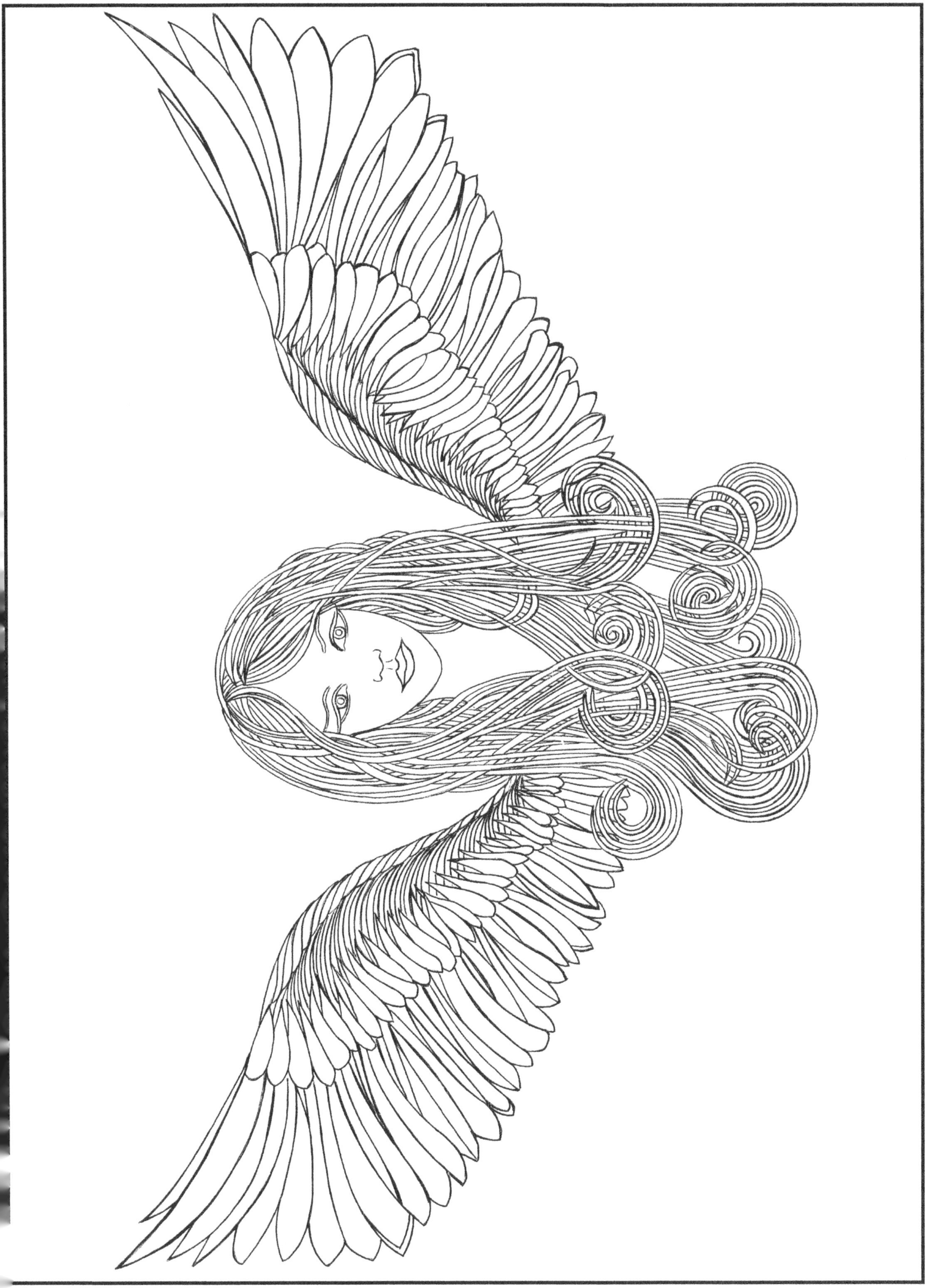

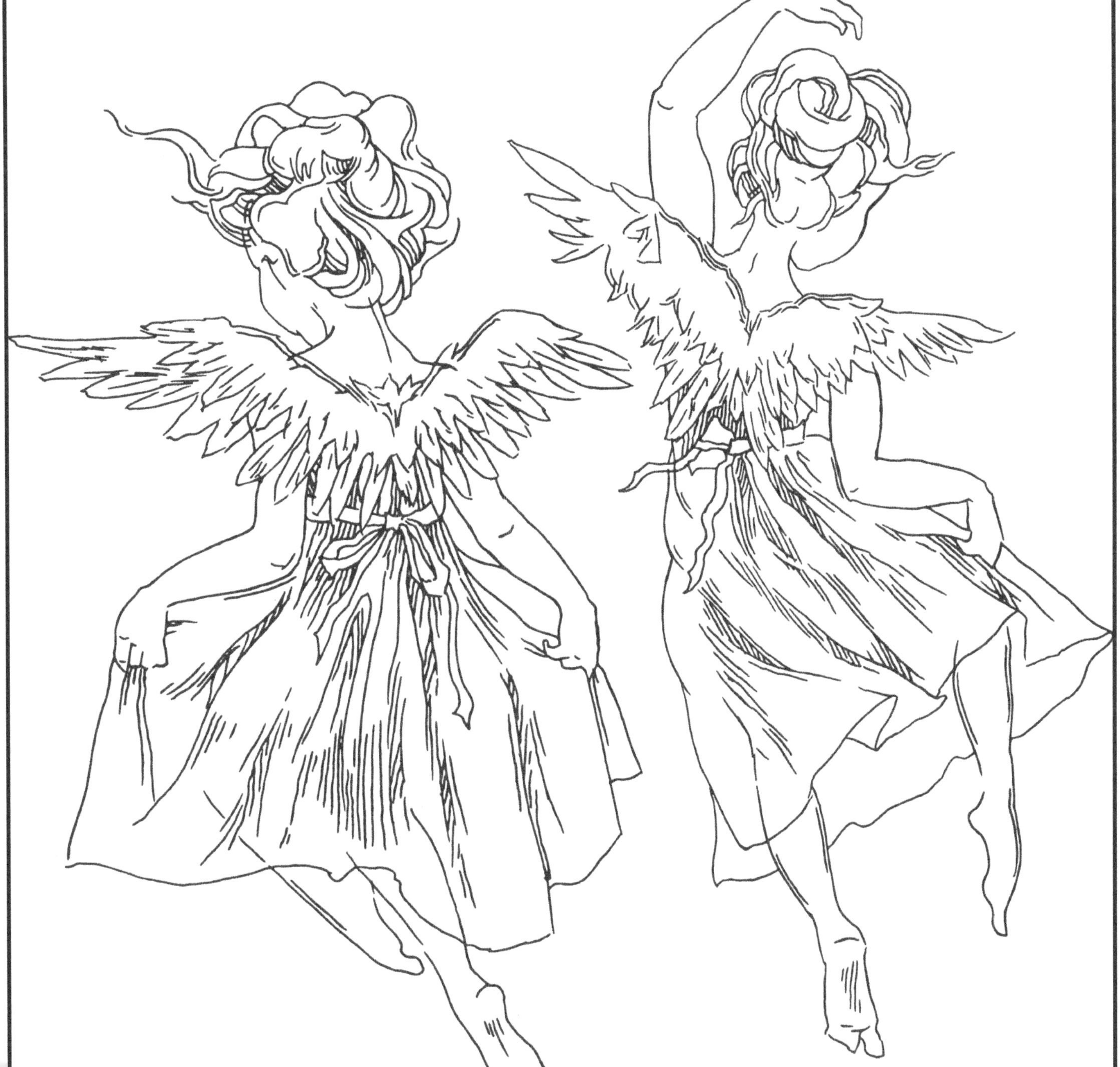

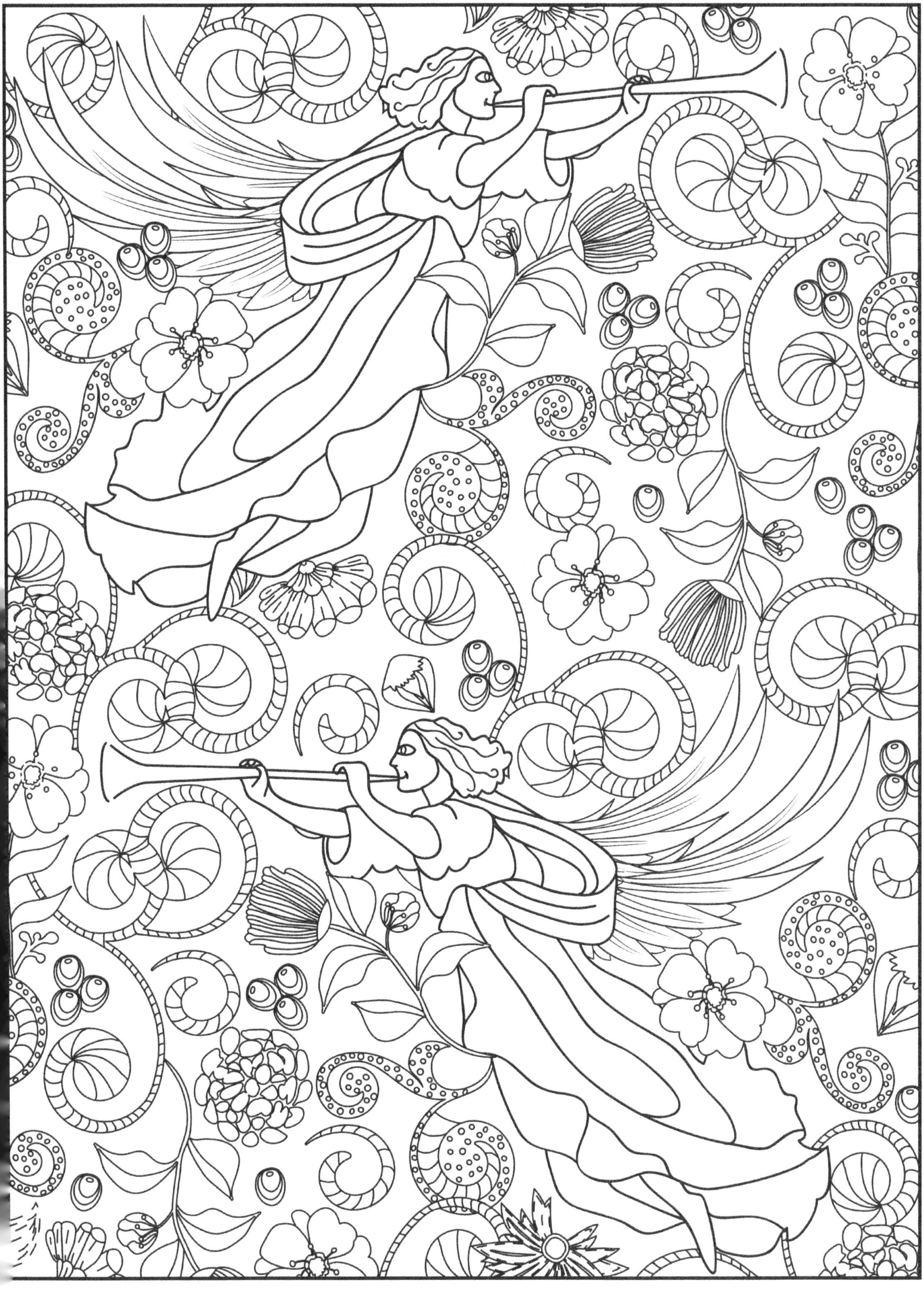

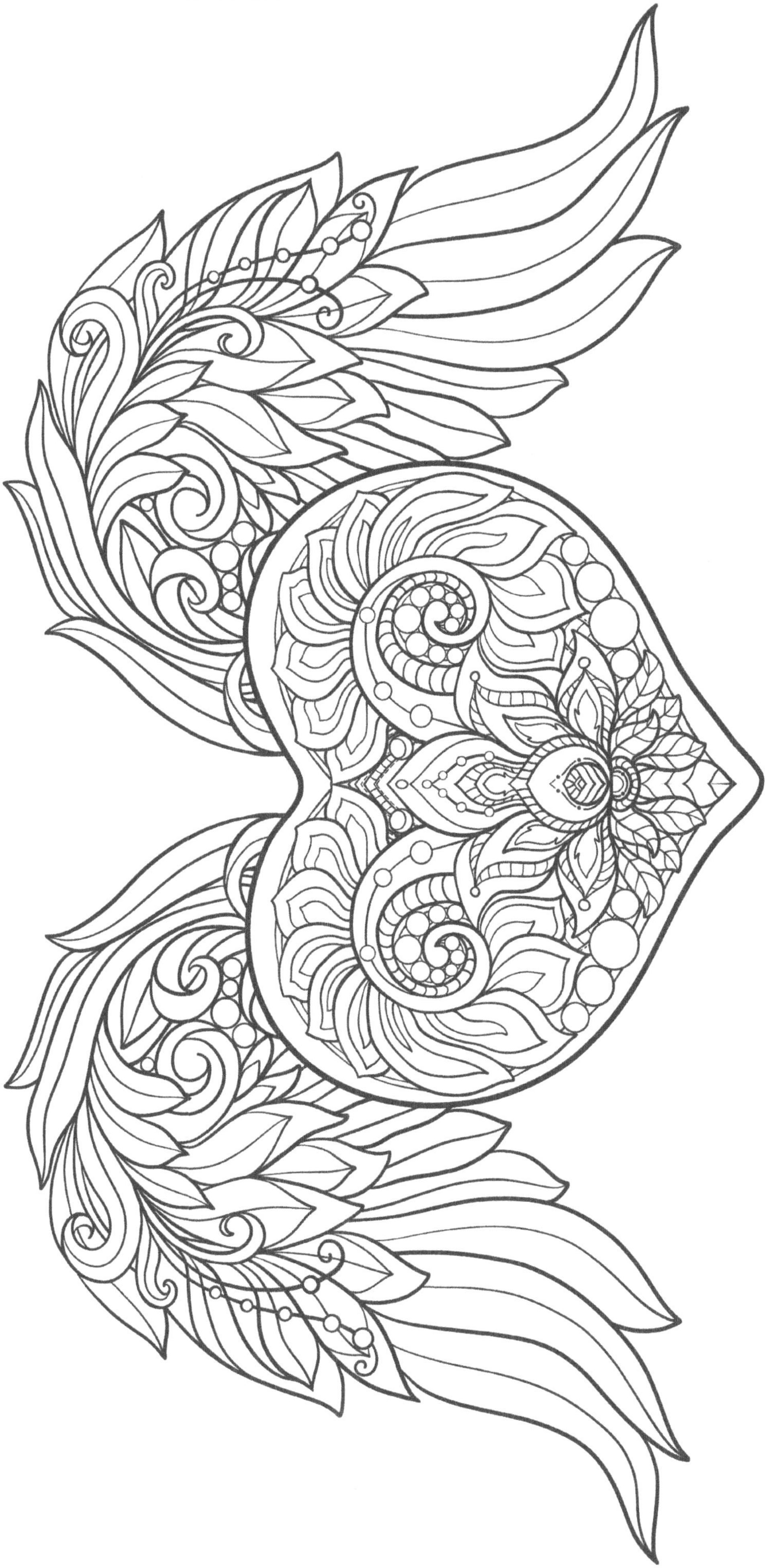

Made in the USA
Coppell, TX
16 February 2023

12954094R00057